The

Southern Way

The regular volume for the Southern devotee

Peter Waller

Issue 70

ISBN 9781800353411

First published in 2025 by Crécy Publishing Ltd

Contact details
All editorial submissions to:
The Southern Way
Crécy Publishing Limited
1a Ringway Trading Estate
Shadowmoss Road
Manchester M22 5LL
enquiries@crecy.co.uk

A CIP record for this book is available from the British Library

Publisher's note: Every effort has been made to identify and correctly attribute photographic credits. Any error that may have occurred is entirely unintentional.

FSC MIX Paper | Supporting responsible forestry FSC® C014540

Printed in the UK by Short Run Press

Crécy Publishing Limited
1a Ringway Trading Estate
Shadowmoss Road
Manchester M22 5LH

www.crecy.co.uk

Front cover:
On 18 September 1961 'King Arthur' class 4-6-0 No 30451 *Sir Lamorak* is pictured heading west at Deepcut with the 2.54pm service from Waterloo to Basingstoke. Allocated to Salisbury since 1950, by the date of the photograph the 4-6-0 was the last of the Class G14 rebuilds to remain in service; it was finally withdrawn in mid-June 1962 having outlived the penultimate in the batch — No 30453 *King Arthur* — by almost a year. See the article on the class on pages 5-23.
Alexander McBlain/Online

Back cover:
As Class 444 No 444003 departs with an Up service from Basingstoke, Class 159 No 159005 approaches from the east with a Down service on 11 May 2017.
Gavin Morrison

Title page:
On 4 March 1989 Class 419 MLV No 9009 stands at London Bridge station, where it had been stranded due to an accident at Purley. *Alex Dasi-Sutton*

Contents

Introduction

The current year marks the bicentenary of the use of steam power — courtesy of *Locomotion* — to haul a passenger train. *Public Domain*

These words are being penned just over halfway through a year that is being marketed as 'Railway 200' and at the time when the 'Great Gathering' at Derby is at the forefront of many enthusiasts' minds. The year and the event will undoubtedly help to raise the profile of the railway and is history but, what exactly, does the 200 years mark?

The origins of the railway in the British Isles stretches back much further than 1825. The first recorded wagonways appeared in the later 17th century; the first line to be constructed using an Act of Parliament was the Middleton Railway that received its Act in 1757; the first railway to operate a passenger service was the Oystermouth in 1807; and, in terms of steam traction, there were a number of examples that predated *Locomotion* on the Stockton & Darlington through the work of, inter alia, Richard Trevithick, John Blenkinsop and George Stephenson himself. And yet 1825 has acquired almost a mythical status. What claim to fame does the Stockton & Darlington actually have (other than the fact that the use of *Locomotion* represented the first use of a steam locomotive to haul passengers on a public railway)? It was effectively the railway that launched the North Eastern Railway, one of the most significant of the pre-grouping companies and one that had recently been subsumed into the LNER when its centenary arose in 1925. Of all the pre-grouping companies the NER seems to have valued its history more than many of its contemporaries. In 1875 the NER had marked the 50th anniversary of the S&DR and, through the efforts of J. B. Harper, it had started to put historic items of rolling stock aside from the 1880s with a view to their preservation. A number of these were to feature in the centenary events that marked the Stockton & Darlington's centenary in 1925 and were also to form the core of the first railway museum to be established at York three years later.

The date of the 1925 celebrations — July — was selected not to reflect the actual centenary of the first use of *Locomotion* on a passenger train — which was in late September 1825 — but for the convenience of international visitors to the International Railway Congress held that year to attend. Some 130 delegates to the congress, representing most of the world with the exception of Germany and Russia, arrived in the UK in June 1925 with the centenary celebrations very much to the forefront of their plans. A hundred years later, the Greatest Gathering was held over three days at the start of August; in 1975, the cavalcade to mark the 150th anniversary took place on 31 August following a week long exhibition at Shildon. Even the date of the actual anniversary seems to be flexible.

The bicentenary of the Stockton & Darlington is certainly worthy of celebration but it could be argued that we're really marking the success of the NER in creating the story that it was the cradle of the railway revolution.

Peter Waller

The 'King Arthur' class

Prior to the outbreak of the First World War Robert Urie designed the Class H15 4-6-0 for the LSWR; the first of the type was completed in December 1913 and trials indicated that the basic design had the potential with modifications to provide a new class of powerful express locomotive capable of operating services over the main line west from Basingstoke towards Salisbury and Exeter.

With Britain at war, the project to produce new express passenger locomotives took a back seat and it was not until 1917 that Urie undertook the design for what became the Class N15 4-6-0. Although there were similarities to the 'H15', there were also significant changes. The diameter of the driving wheels was increased from 6ft 0in to 6ft 7in, the cylinders were also larger (22in x 28in as opposed to 21in x 28in, making them the largest employed on any British steam locomotive at the time) and the boiler was tapered rather than parallel (the first time that tapered boilers had been constructed at Eastleigh).

Wartime conditions and restrictions on the use of raw materials delayed the actual construction of the locomotives until authorisation was received in mid-1918 and the first of the initial batch of 10 — No 736 — emerged from Eastleigh Works in the summer of 1918, entering service on 31 August. All 10 of the initial batch, Nos 736-45, were completed by November 1919 with the last quintet being delayed slightly as result of problems in obtaining the copper required. Production of a second batch — Nos 746-55 — was undertaken at Eastleigh between June 1922 and March 1923, with the last three of the batch emerging after the LSWR had been subsumed into the Southern.

The origins of the 'King Arthur' class lay in Urie's earlier Class H15 4-6-0 of which the initial 10 — Nos 482-91 — were constructed at Eastleigh between December 1913 and July 1914. As a youthful admirer looks on, here No 30486 — one of eight of the class withdrawn during 1959 — is seen entering Vauxhall station with a Down service. This particular locomotive was allocated to Nine Elms for its entire BR career. *J. Joyce/Online Transport Archive*

A view of Urie-designed No 736 when new in the summer of 1918. The first 20 locomotives — Nos 736-55 — were poor steamers and, in 1924, they were modified in order to improve performance. Despite this work, they were never the equal of the newer locomotives and, it is said, Maunsell was displeased when the Southern decided to allocate names to them as part of the 'King Arthur' class, allegedly commenting that 'names would not improve their performance'. The locomotive is seen with the eight-wheel 5,000 gallon tender that was standard to this batch when delivered; the LSWR required larger capacity tenders for use on long distance routes as it forswore the use of water troughs. When the Urie 'N15s' were withdrawn, many of the tenders survived to be reused with the later batches. *Crécy Archive*

Although undated, this view of No E763 *Sir Bors de Ganis* must be from the period between its naming after the SR decided to allocate names to all express passenger locomotives and June 1928 when it received smoke deflectors. One of the 'Scotch Arthurs', built by North British, No E763 entered service in May 1925 and was allocated to Stewarts Lane for the first decade of its operational career. It was to remain on the South Eastern until 1955 when it was transferred to Basingstoke on the South Western. *Crécy Archive*

When initially fitted with smoke deflectors in September 1926, No E772 *Sir Percivale* was equipped with German-pattern ones; these were to survive on the locomotive for more than six years as it was not until October 1932 that the locomotive received standard pattern deflectors — the last of the class to be so fitted. *Crécy Archive*

In the late summer of 1940 No 783 *Sir Gillemere* was modified; three small diameter stovepipe chimneys replaced its single chimney. The work was undertaken as part of an experiment to see if it was possible to reduce the visibility of locomotives to Luftwaffe crews during the early months of the Second World War. This change was not to last long, however, as in November 1940 the three chimneys were replaced by two larger diameter stovepipe chimneys as illustrated by this view of the locomotive at Eastleigh taken on 7 January 1941. A month or so later the locomotive reverted to a single standard chimney. *B. W. Anwell*

It is post-nationalisation — the date is 22 May 1948 — as No 775 *Sir Agravaine* speeds through Tonbridge with an Up special boat train. The locomotive still bears its Southern number and is in Southern malachite green livery; it would not be until November 1949 that the locomotive would emerge renumbered and repainted into BR green. Allocated to Stewarts Lane when pictured here, the locomotive was reallocated to Dover Marine in February 1951 and then to Feltham in mid-June 1959. It was finally withdrawn less than a year later, in February 1960. *John Meredith/Online Transport Archive*

An undated view — but one that can possibly be ascribed to late 1948 as the locomotive first emerged bearing its BR number and livery in October that year — sees No 30451 *Sir Lamorak* look in ex-works condition. At the time the locomotive retained its Drummond 'watercart' tender; this was replaced by a tender transferred from Class N15X No 32333 in January 1957. Based at Salisbury from January 1933 until withdrawal at the end of June 1962, except for a brief period between January 1949 and December 1950 when it was based at Basingstoke and then Nine Elms, No 30451 was one of only 12 from the class to survive into 1962. *J. Jarvis/Online Transport Archive*

With Richard Maunsell appointed by the Southern in 1923, the new CME had plans for new express designs for the company. However, there would be a time lag before these locomotives could be introduced and, in the meantime, there was a requirement for additional express locomotives for the summer timetable in 1925. This was achieved through the notional rebuilding of Drummond's Classes G14 (Nos 453-57) and P14 (Nos 448-52); very little of the original locomotives, however, survived into the completed locomotives although the 'new' locomotives inherited the tenders from the earlier 'G14s' and 'P14s'. This third batch was modified from the earlier two batches largely through the influence of Maunsell himself and of his chief draughtman, James Clayton, both of whom had been privy to developments in steam locomotive design elsewhere through their wartime connections.

The third batch — Nos 448-57 — all entered service between February and July 1925. Based on trials the previous year on No 442, the batch was fitted with smaller diameter cylinders — 20½in — but with the pressure in the Urie-designed boilers increased from 180psi to 200psi. In addition the Eastleigh pattern superheater was replaced by that designed by Maunsell with a larger steam chest and an increased diameter chimney. This batch retained the Drummond pattern cab.

Recognising that even with the 10 rebuilds available there would still be a shortage of express locomotives, and lacking capacity in its own workshops, the SR ordered a further batch of 20 'N15s' from the Glasgow-based North British Locomotive Co Ltd in December 1924; the order was subsequently increased to 30 with all being delivered between April and October 1925. Nos 763-92 — nicknamed the 'Scotch Arthurs' as a result of their provenance — differed from the earlier locomotives in being built to the SR's composite loading gauge and thus incorporating the Ashford-style cab, which permitted the type's use over most of the restricted routes on the South Eastern.

The 'Scotch Arthurs' were initially to prove disappointing in service when introduced. Those on the South Eastern resulted in no improvement in performance over the ex-SECR 4-4-0s they were designed to replace with issues relating to hot boxes, defects in boiler construction and poor steaming. Investigation identified major problems with quality of the workmanship at North British — largely the consequence of the company being so desperate for the work that the price was underquoted. A considerable amount of work was required, undertaken at Eastleigh following a report in 1926, to improve the condition of the batch.

In May 1925 a final batch of 25 'N15s', Nos 793-817, was ordered for operation on the Central and Eastern sections; however, production of the type ceased after No E806 *Sir Galleron* was completed at Eastleigh in January 1927 with additional 'Lord Nelsons' being constructed in their place. The intention was to equip Nos 793-807 with 4,000 gallon six-wheel tenders for use primarily on boat train duties in place of Nos 763-72 as the latter's 5,000 gallon tenders were considered more suitable for use on the Western Section's longer routes. The undelivered locomotives from this batch were planned to receive 3,500 gallon tenders, as used on the 'N' class, for use on the Central Section, which had shorter turntables. With the cancellation of this final batch, 'N' class tenders were allocated to Nos 793-806; however, before these could be used, the frames beneath the cabs of the locomotives had to be modified in order to accommodate the higher draw-gear that the tenders used.

Opposite top: **In April 1950 the pioneer of the rebuilt Drummond locomotives, No 30453 *King Arthur*, is pictured on Basingstoke shed. At this date the locomotive had only recently received its BR identity — two months earlier in fact, although it had originally emerged in BR livery bearing the number S453 in February 1948 — and was allocated to Salisbury. It was to spend its entire BR career based there before withdrawal in July 1961.** *Neil Davenport/Online Transport Archive*

Bottom: **In early 1949, presumably in February when the locomotive was renumbered, No 30736 emerged with vertical smoke deflectors as illustrated here. The date is 3 January 1951 and the locomotive is providing the motive power on the 12.25pm local service from Weymouth to Bournemouth Central when recorded at Creekmoor Junction. Based at Bournemouth shed for the bulk of its BR career, the locomotive was withdrawn in early November 1956.** *J. B. Herman*

Looking very smart in ex-works condition in its new BR livery is No 30456 *Sir Galahad*, the 4-6-0 would soon be released back to traffic at Salisbury shed, where it was based at nationalisation. Five of the class — Nos 30453-57 — were notional rebuilds of the earlier Class G14 4-6-0s and inherited the Drummond-designed eight-wheel 'watercart' 4,300 gallon tenders used on the older locomotives. Over the years these tenders proved problematic; the inside bearings were inadequate for the loads carried and suffered from water ingress. The withdrawal of the Urie batch of the class in the mid-1950s released the eight-wheel tenders used on this batch and these were used to replace the 'watercart' tenders on Nos 448-57. Between 1953 and the late spring of 1956 No 30456 was allocated to Nine Elms before returning to Salisbury. A final move — in early 1957 — saw the 4-6-0 transferred to Basingstoke from where it was withdrawn in mid-May 1960. *John Meredith/Online Transport Archive*

30453

30736

Pictured approaching Sturry on 2 April 1953 with the 11.28am service from Ashford to Margate is No 30804 *Sir Cador of Cornwall*. A South Eastern locomotive for the bulk of its BR career — being based at Ashford initially and then Dover from mid-1957 — No 30804 was one of the class transferred to the South Western — at Eastleigh shed — in June 1959 as a result of the Kent Coast electrification scheme. It was withdrawn from Eastleigh in mid-February 1962. *Donald Kelk/Online Transport Archive*

Contemporaneously with the construction of the later batches of the class, the SR's board decided in early 1925 to adopt the policy of naming the locomotives employed on express passenger locomotives. With its connections to the West Country and the employment of the class on West of England services, names associated with the legend of King Arthur were selected, at the suggestion of John Elliot (the SR's Public Relations Officer), with the first — *King Arthur* — being allocated to No E453.

Following complaints from the crews over visibility, Maunsell investigated the use of smoke deflectors. The Southern was the first railway in Britain to look at this embellishment and Maunsell was influenced by work in Germany. In all six locomotives — Nos E453, E457, E753, E772, E774 and E783 — all received experimental modifications between 1926 and 1929 but it was E772 *Sir Percivale* that saw the first use of full-height deflectors (to a German design) when it was modified. The eventual design adopted by Maunsell was subtly different to that on No E772 and all were so equipped in October 1932.

The class was initially designed to operate on the main line towards the south-west; until 1922, when the line west of Salisbury was upgraded, the class only ran as far as Salisbury. With the grouping and the construction of the later batches, the areas of operation expanded considerably to encompass the Central and Eastern as well, including services to and from the Channel ports. When the 'Bournemouth Belle' was launched on 5 July 1931 the locomotive used on the inaugural run was No E780 *Sir Persant*. In early 1943 10 examples of the class — Nos 739/40/42/44/47-51/54 — were to be found well away from their traditional haunts; transferred to Heaton shed, in Newcastle upon Tyne, the locomotives were utilised on a range of passenger and freight traffic in north-east England and southern Scotland until the summer of the same year when they were returned to the Southern, having been replaced by USATC Class S160 2-8-0s. After nationalisation, the class was increasingly concentrated on the South Western; this process was largely completed in 1959 following the first phase of the Kent Coast electrification, which saw the class supplanted on their remaining duties in the area.

On 16 July 1955 No 30787 *Sir Menadeuke* is seen entering Salisbury station. Based on the South Western for its entire operational life, the locomotive had been based at Eastleigh from early February 1951. It was withdrawn from that shed at the end of February eight years later.
Bernard Harrison/Online Transport Archive

Bearing its 73B — Bricklayers Arms — shed code, No 30799 *Sir Ironside* is recorded here between Herne Bay and Birchington on 13 September 1953 with the 9.8am Bricklayers Arms to Ramsgate via Woolwich Arsenal summer Sundays service. Based at the London shed for the bulk of its BR career, No 30799 was another of the class to be transferred to the South Western — this time to Salisbury (from where it was withdrawn in late February 1961) — in June 1959. *Donald Kelk/Online Transport Archive*

In terms of livery, the 'Urie Arthurs' originally appeared in LSWR olive green livery; after the grouping, these and subsequent locomotives emerged in Maunsell green (with varying styles of lining). In 1939, following the appointment of Bulleid as CME, locomotives started to appear in either olive or malachite green (again in the latter case with variants in terms of lining). During the Second World War locomotives appeared in either malachite green (up to March 1942) or in black (from April 1942 until January 1946); the first to emerge in the latter livery was No 456. In March 1946 the use of malachite green was resumed and the last locomotive to be repainted in this livery was No 30786, post-nationalisation, in July 1949. The first of the class to appear in BR dark green was No 30783 later the same month. All of the class had been repainted in BR green by the end of December 1952; the last to emerge in the new livery was No 30786.

Following the grouping, the existing locomotives and those constructed post-1923 received an 'E' prefix before their running numbers; this policy was abandoned in the early 1930s when the ex-SECR locomotives were renumbered in the 31xxx series and the ex-LBSCR ones 32xxx. At nationalisation, a number of ex-Southern locomotives were initially to appear with an 'S' prefix. This was carried by five of the 'King Arthurs': Nos 453, 747/50/53 plus 754 very briefly. The process of renumbering the locomotives in the 30xxx series commenced in May 1948; this was completed in July 1951 when No 30770 *Sir Prianius* emerged sporting its new number.

The beginning of the end of the class came shortly after nationalisation. Initially, the 'Urie N15s' were deemed surplus to requirements during the winter months between 1949 and 1952 and placed into store. Resurrected for summer services, the class was to suffer its first withdrawal in 1953 when No 30754 was withdrawn due to cracked frames. All of the 'Urie N15s' were withdrawn by early March 1958; their names were reallocated to BR Standard Class 5s. The Kent Coast electrification allied to the increased availability of BR Standard designs saw the later locomotives taken out of service; the last to remain operational was No 30770 *Sir Prianius*, which was withdrawn in November 1962. Although there were plans to preserve No 30453, these proved impractical and, as a result, No 30777 *Sir Lamiel* was selected to became part of the national collection. A frequent performer on the main line following the lifting of the steam ban, No 30777 has been based on the Great Central Railway since 1986 although its most recent boiler certificate expired in 2017. At the time of writing the locomotive is undergoing a major overhaul in order to return it to steam.

Class N15

No.	Name	New	Smoke deflectors fitted	BR No. and date	Withdrawn	Notes
448	*Sir Tristram*	May 1925	February 1929	30448 July 1948	August 1960	Received tender from No 30478 in May 1955
449	*Sir Torre*	June 1925	April 1929	30449 October 1949	December 1959	Displayed at the centenary of the Stockton & Darlington Railway in July 1925; received tender from No 30753 in November 1955
450	*Sir Kay*	June 1925	December 1927	30450 October 1949	September 1960	Received tender from No 30737 in October 1956
451	*Sir Lamorak*	June 1925	November 1927	30451 July 1948	June 1962	Received tender from No 32333 in January 1957
452	*Sir Meliagrance*	July 1925	December 1927	30452 May 1948	August 1959	Received tender from No 30785 in June 1957
453	*King Arthur*	February 1925	April 1927 (small); July 1928 (standard)	30453 February 1950	July 1961	Received tender from No 30742 in April 1957; identified for preservation in November 1960 and stored initially after withdrawal; the decision to restore the locomotive to an 'as-built' condition and the lack of a suitable Drummond watercart tender resulted in No 453 being rejected in place of No 777. No 453 was scrapped in October 1961.
454	*Queen Guinevere*	March 1925	July 1928	30454 April 1949	October 1958	Received tender from No 456 in July 1946 and from No 30755 in June 1957
455	*Sir Launcelot*	March 1925	March 1928	30455 May 1948	April 1959	Received tender from No 30748 in December 1957
456	*Sir Galahad*	April 1925	March 1928	30456 October 1948	May 1960	Received tender from No 454 in July 1946 and from No 30749 in August 1958
457	*Sir Bedivere*	April 1925	February 1928	30457 August 1949	May 1961	Received tender from No 30490 in June 1955
736	*Excalibur*	August 1918	September 1928 (standard); January 1949 (vertical)	30736 March 1949	October 1956	Fitted with Lemaître multiple jet exhaust January 1941; retained until withdrawal
737	*King Uther*	October 1918	June 1928	30737 July 1949	August 1956	Converted to oil burning in April to September 1921 and again briefly during the General Strike of 1926; fitted with Lemaître multiple jet exhaust February 1941; retained until withdrawal
738	*King Pellinore*	December 1918	July 1928	30738 May 1949	March 1958	
739	*King Leodegrance*	February 1919	January 1928	30739 March 1949	May 1957	Allocated to Heaton (LNER) between January and September 1943; converted to oil burning in June to August 1921 (burst into flames at Salisbury shed on 28 July 1921) and again briefly during the General Strike of 1926
740	*Merlin*	April 1919	May 1928	30740 November 1948	December 1955	Allocated to Heaton (LNER) between January and September 1943; converted to oil burning between 1946/47 and 1948

No.	Name	New	Smoke deflectors fitted	BR No. and date	Withdrawn	Notes
741	*Joyous Gard*	May 1919	January 1928	30741 December 1948	February 1956	Fitted with Lemaître multiple jet exhaust January 1941; retained until withdrawal
742	*Camelot*	June 1919	June 1928	30742 November 1948	February 1957	Allocated to Heaton (LNER) between January and September 1943
743	*Lyonesse*	August 1919	November 1927	30743 June 1949	October 1955	
744	*Maid of Astolat*	September 1919	November 1927	30744 May 1948	January 1956	Allocated to Heaton (LNER) between January and July 1943
745	*Tintagel*	November 1919	July 1928	30745 December 1948	February 1956	Converted to oil burning between 1946/47 and 1948
746	*Pendragon*	June 1922	January 1929	30746 November 1950	November 1955	
747	*Elaine*	July 1922	August 1928	30747 May 1950	October 1956	Allocated to Heaton (LNER) between January and July 1943
748	*Vivien*	August 1922	November 1929	30748 December 1948	September 1957	Allocated to Heaton (LNER) between January and July 1943; converted to oil burning between 1946/47 and 1948
749	*Iseult*	September 1922	August 1927	30749 December 1948	June 1957	Allocated to Heaton (LNER) between January and July 1943; converted to oil burning between 1946/47 and 1948
750	*Morgan Le Fay*	October 1922	January 1928	30750 December 1948	July 1957	Allocated to Heaton (LNER) between January and July 1943
751	*Etarre*	November 1922	December 1928	30751 July 1948	June 1957	Suffered bomb damage in 1940 when Nine Elms shed hit; allocated to Heaton (LNER) between January and July 1943
752	*Linette*	December 1922	December 1927	30752 September 1948	December 1955	Converted to oil burning between 1946/47 and 1948; fitted with Lemaître multiple jet exhaust January 1941; retained until withdrawal
753	*Melisande*	January 1923	January 1928	30753 May 1948	March 1957	Involved in a collision with No 860 at Farnborough on 26 November 1947; two people were killed
754	*The Green Knight*	February 1923	July 1928	30754 July 1948	February 1953	Allocated to Heaton (LNER) between January and July 1943; received tender from No 30755 in February 1953 (for scrap purposes only)
755	*The Red Knight*	March 1923	January 1928 (standard); February 1945 (vertical)	30755 1949	May 1957	Fitted with Lemaître multiple jet exhaust February 1940; retained until withdrawal; suffered bomb damage in 1940 when Nine Elms shed hit; received tender from No 30754 in February 1953
763	*Sir Bors de Ganis*	May 1925	June 1928	30763 August 1950	September 1960	Tender replaced in 1928 and 1936 and received tender from No 32330 in February 1956
764	*Sir Gawain*	May 1925	April 1928	30764 March 1949	July 1961	Tender replaced in 1928 and 1936
765	*Sir Gareth*	May 1925	November 1927	30765 April 1949	September 1962	Tender replaced in 1928 and 1936 and received tender from No 30767 in November 1959

No.	Name	New	Smoke deflectors fitted	BR No. and date	Withdrawn	Notes
766	*Sir Geraint*	May 1925	February 1928	30766 January 1949	December 1958	Tender replaced in 1929 and 1939 and received tender from No 788 in March 1945
767	*Sir Valence*	June 1925	April 1928	30767 December 1948	June 1959	Tender replaced in 1930 and 1937
768	*Sir Balin*	June 1925	June 1928	30768 November 1948	October 1961	Tender replaced in 1928, 1930 and 1932
769	*Sir Balan*	June 1925	March 1928	30769 April 1951	February 1960	Tender replaced in 1929 and 1931
770	*Sir Prianius*	June 1925	March 1928	30770 July 1951	November 1962	Tender replaced in 1928, 1930 and 1932; on 18 September 1962 the locomotive was hauling a five-coach newspaper train near Botley when four of the carriages were destroyed by fire.
771	*Sir Sagramore*	June 1925	October 1928	30771 June 1950	March 1961	Tender replaced in 1928, 1930 and 1931
772	*Sir Percivale*	June 1925	September 1926 (German pattern); October 1932 (standard)	30772 May 1948	September 1961	Tender replaced in 1929, 1930 and 1931
773	*Sir Lavaine*	June 1925	December 1927	30773 July 1948	February 1962	
774	*Sir Gaheris*	June 1925	June 1927	30774 June 1925	January 1960	
775	*Sir Agravaine*	June 1925	December 1927	30775 October 1949	February 1960	Suffered bomb damage in 1940 when Nine Elms shed hit
776	*Sir Galagars*	June 1925	December 1927	30776 July 1949	January 1959	
777	*Sir Lamiel*	June 1925	December 1927	30777 May 1948	October 1961	Preserved
778	*Sir Pelleas*	June 1925	January 1928	30778 November 1949	May 1959	
July 1959779		*Sir Colgrevance*	July 1925	April 1927 November 1948	30779	
780	*Sir Persant*	July 1925	December 1927	30780 January 1950	July 1959	
781	*Sir Aglovale*	July 1925	December 1927	30781 April 1949	May 1962	
782	*Sir Brian*	July 1925	October 1927	30782 May 1948	September 1962	
783	*Sir Gillemere*	August 1925	December 1927	30783 May 1948	February 1961	Modified stovepipe chimneys installed late 1940 until February 1941; involved in a collision at Bournemouth Central on 22 January 1955 with No 30485
784	*Sir Nerovens*	August 1925	January 1928	30784 May 1948	October 1959	
785	*Sir Mador de la Porte*	August 1925	February 1928	30785 August 1948	October 1959	Received tender from No 30746 in April 1957 and from No 30791 in November 1959 (after withdrawal)
786	*Sir Lionel*	August 1925	Late 1927	30786 September 1948	August 1959	
787	*Sir Menadeuke*	September 1925	November 1927	30787 April 1949	February 1959	
788	*Sir Urre of the Mount*	September 1925	December 1927	30788 November 1948	February 1962	Tender replaced March 1944

No.	Name	New	Smoke deflectors fitted	BR No. and date	Withdrawn	Notes
789	*Sir Guy*	September 1925	August 1928	30789 August 1948	December 1959	
790	*Sir Villiars*	September 1925	February 1928	30790 September 1948	October 1961	
791	*Sir Uwaine*	September 1925	January 1928	30791 December 1948	May 1960	Received tender from No 30785 in November 1959
792	*Sir Hervis de Revel*	October 1925	April 1928	30792 March 1950	February 1959	Fitted with Lemaître multiple jet exhaust January 1941; removed March 1952
793	*Sir Ontzlake*	March 1926	April 1929	30793 November 1948	September 1962	Received tender from No 30776 in September 1959
794	*Sir Ector de Maris*	March 1926	May 1928	30794 January 1949	August 1960	Received tender from No 30795 in September 1958
795	*Sir Dinadan*	April 1926	January 1930	30795 April 1949	July 1962	Received tender from No 30800 in December 1953 and from No 30738 in April 1958
796	*Sir Dodinas le Savage*	May 1926	February 1931	30796 February 1950	February 1962	Received tender from No 30766 in January 1961
797	*Sir Blamor de Ganis*	June 1926	January 1929	30797 January 1949	June 1959	
798	*Sir Hectimere*	June 1926	November 1927	30798 November 1949	June 1962	Received tender from No 30450 in October 1960
799	*Sir Ironside*	July 1926	July 1930	30799 May 1948	February 1961	
800	*Sir Meleaus de Lile*	September 1926	November 1927	30800 October 1949	August 1961	Received tender from No 30795 in December 1953 and from No 30454 in January 1959
801	*Sir Meliot de Logres*	October 1926	February 1928	30801 July 1949	April 1959	Received tender from No 30800 in December 1958
802	*Sir Durnore*	October 1926	September 1928	30802 July 1948	July 1961	Received tender from No 30806 in February 1955 and from 30750 in June 1958
803	*Sir Harry le Fise Lake*	November 1926	March 1928	30803 July 1948	August 1961	Received tender from No 30792 in November 1959
804	*Sir Cador of Cornwall*	December 1926	October 1928	30804 December 1948	February 1961	
805	*Sir Constantine*	January 1927	December 1928	30805 September 1948	November 1959	
806	*Sir Galleron*	January 1927	April 1928	30806 September 1948	April 1961	Damaged by a V1 flying bomb when train it was hauling at Upchurch was hit on 16 August 1944. Eight people were killed as a result of the attack; received tender from No 32331 in August 1958

Opposite top: **On 22 May 1956 'Urie Arthur' No 30751 *Etarre* is pictured heading west at Deepcut with a Waterloo to Basingstoke local. When recorded here the locomotive was still allocated to Nine Elms, where it had been based since May 1951 but was to be transferred to Basingstoke — its final shed — in mid-June 1956. It was to survive in service for a further year before withdrawal in mid-June 1957. Its eight-wheel tender was not one of those reallocated following withdrawal of the locomotive.** *Alexander McBlain/Online Transport Archive*

Bottom: **Although undated, this view of No 30449 *Sir Torre* must have been taken after November 1955 as it was in that month that the locomotive received the eight-wheel tender from withdrawn No 30753 in place of its original Drummond-designed eight-wheel 'watercart' tender. Nos 30448-52 were notional rebuilds in 1925 of the five Class P14 4-6-0s constructed to a design of Dugald Drummond and completed at Eastleigh Works in 1910.** *J. Joyce/Online Transport Archive*

30751

30449
30449
7

30803
340

RCTS
30796
RCTS
RCTS

The last of the class to be completed — No 30806 *Sir Galleron* — is seen here departing from Faversham with the 11.35am service from Victoria to Ramsgate on 16 March 1959. By this date, operation of the class on the South Eastern was drawing to a close — as evinced by the newly installed but still unused third rail — as redundancy, as a result of the Kent Coast electrification, was only three months away. No 30806 was allocated to Ashford at the start of its BR career; it was also to spend time allocated to Dover Marine and Hither Green before it was transferred to the South Western in June 1959. It was withdrawn from Eastleigh in late April 1961. *Alexander McBlain/Online Transport Archive*

Opposite top: Pictured passing through Hither Green station during 1957 is No 30803 *Sir Harry le Fise Lake*. Allocated to Ashford since March 1944, the engine was still operating with its original six-wheel tender when recorded here; it was to receive an eight-wheel tender from withdrawn No 30792 in early November 1959. By that date, following the Kent Coast electrification, it had been transferred to the South Western and was based at Eastleigh through to withdrawal in early September 1961. *Fred Ivey/Online Transport Archive*

Bottom: On 13 April 1958, the RCTS organised its 'Sussex Coast Limited' railtour which saw Atlantic No 32424 operate its final duty prior to withdrawal on the outbound leg from Victoria to Newhaven Harbour. The return journey from Brighton to Victoria was hauled by No 30796 *Sir Dodinas le Savage*, still with its original six-wheel Ashford 3,500 gallon tender, and the locomotive, looking in excellent condition, is pictured here shortly before its booked departure time of 4.16pm. At the time of the tour the locomotive was allocated to Hither Green, a shed that had a reputation for caring well for its allocated 'King Arthurs'. It was reallocated to Salisbury — its final shed — in June 1961 and, in January 1961, received a replacement tender from No 30766. This was the last locomotive in the class to undergo a tender change. No 30796 was withdrawn in early March 1962. *John McCann/Online Transport Archive*

At about 12.15pm on 29 August 1959, No 30764 *Sir Gawain* was one of three locomotives pictured heading light engine from Waterloo to Nine Elms. Based on the South Western from early July 1955, when it was reallocated to Eastleigh (and based there for about a month), No 30764 was to spend the bulk of its later BR career based at Bournemouth from where it was withdrawn in late July 1961. *Fred Ivey/Online Transport Archive*

Opposite top: **A contrast in styles at Clapham Junction in 1959 sees No 30448 *Sir Tristram* approach the station with a Down service whilst Unrebuilt 'West Country' No 34044, which was rebuilt in May the following year, awaits departure with an Up service and Rebuilt 'Merchant Navy' No 35009 *Shaw Savill* potters through light engine. No 30448, which received a replacement tender from Class H15 No 30478 in May 1955, was allocated to only two sheds for its entire operational life: Exmouth Junction from new in May 1925 and then Salisbury from May 1949 until withdrawal at the end of August 1960.** *Fred Ivey/Online Transport Archive*

Bottom: **On 31 December 1960 No 30765 *Sir Gareth* is seen heading east at Potbridge, near Winchfield, with the Saturdays Only 1.16pm service from Eastleigh to Waterloo. A well-travelled locomotive — the 4-6-0 was based at no fewer than six sheds on the South Eastern and South Western during its BR career — by the time it was recorded here it was allocated to Basingstoke, from where it was withdrawn in late September 1962.** *Alexander McBlain/Online Transport Archive*

Class 159s to the West

In *Southern Way 68* we explored the operation of the Class 50s on the London to Exeter main line; it is frightening to think that it is now more than 30 years since the Class 159s assumed responsibility for the services over this line. The first of the class was handed over in January 1993. The units had originally been built by BREL at its York Works as part of the programme of Class 150s designed to upgrade the services offered by Regional Railways; however, the sector had over-ordered with the result that the future Class 159s were surplus to requirements. Network SouthEast had a requirement for new rolling stock to replace the locomotive-hauled services on the West of England line and so took on the stock.

A total of 22 units — eventually Nos 159001-22 — were involved. Before these could pass to NSE, a certain amount of remedial work was required to make them suitable for service on the Waterloo-Exeter line. This included the provision of first class accommodation and the installation of retention toilets. In theory, BREL could have taken on this work; however, post its privatisation, BREL was unable to agree terms with NSE for the modifications and so the work was completed by Babcock at Rosyth. The original fleet was supplemented in 2007 by the conversion of redundant Class 158 units from TransPennine Express. These 'new' units became Nos 159101-08. In addition a number of Class 158 two-car sets were also transferred to South West Trains; this allowed the franchisee to operate the service exclusively using Classes 158 and 159 and thus release the nine Class 170 'Turbostar' sets that South West Trains had acquired from 2000 onwards. The latter had proved unsuitable for services through to Exeter as they lacked selective door opening — essential for serving some of the short platforms at stations west of Salisbury — and end gangways (which precluded the operation of trolley services through the train). The nine units concerned were reallocated to TransPennine Express in 2006.

Pictured having just departed from Exeter Central, No 159006 heads east with an Up service on 10 February 1994. *Les Folkard/Online Transport Archive*

The Class 159s remain in service, albeit reduced to only 29 sets following the withdrawal of No 159012 after accident damage. With the recent termination of the South Western Railway franchise, the sets, which are owned since privatisation by Porterbrook, are now in the hands of their fourth operator.

Above: **On 1 June 1994 No 159012 heads west at Surbiton with the 16.05 service from Waterloo to Salisbury.**
Bernard Harrison/Online Transport Archive

On the same day, the pioneer of the class — No 159001 — along with No 159021 form the six-car set for the 17.05 service from Waterloo to Yeovil Junction, which is seen passing through Weybridge on the Down Main. The view shows to good effect the Network SouthEast livery in which the units commenced their operational life.
Bernard Harrison/Online Transport Archive

159013
YW
17
15

On 23 May 2002 No 159004, by now in South West Trains livery, is seen at Exeter Central with the 11.34 service to Waterloo.
Geoffrey Tribe/Online Transport Archive

Opposite top: **On 1 April 1995 No 159021 is pictured again, this time in the company of No 159008, as the pair form the 09.32 service from Yeovil Junction to Waterloo. The train is seen here at Andover.** *Bernard Harrison/Online Transport Archive*

Bottom: **Pictured with a Down service at Basingstoke on 26 July 2001 is No 159013. Although still retaining its Network SouthEast livery at this date, the unit now carries South West Trains branding.** *Geoffrey Tribe/Online Transport Archive*

SOUTH WEST
London Waterloo

159102

No 159102 is pictured again, this time at 11.32.44 on 15 October 2016 at Waterloo, prior to working the 11.50 service to Salisbury. On 31 October 2021 No 159102 was involved in a collision with a Great Western Railway Class 158 at Fisherton Tunnel, Salisbury; this resulted in carriages Nos 57803 and 57803 from No 159102 being written off and subsequently scrapped. *Alex Dasi-Sutton*

Opposite top: **Pictured awaiting departure from Waterloo in early 2003 is No 159005 in full South West Trains livery.** *Harry Luff/Online Transport Archive*

Bottom: **On a December's night — 5 December 2015 to be precise — No 159102 is pictured at Salisbury with the 15.20 service to London Waterloo. This was one of eight 'new' Class 159 units created in 2007 through the rebuilding of redundant Class 158 units that had been replaced by more modern rolling stock on TransPennine Express.** *Alex Dasi-Sutton*

Viewed from the footbridge to the west of the station on 11 April 2017, No 159107 is pictured departing from Woking with a Down service. *Gavin Morrison*

Opposite top: **On the same day, No 158019 rushes through Weybridge on the Up Main as a fast Down service approaches from the east.** *Gavin Morrison*

Bottom: **Another of the ex-TransPennine Express sets — No 159103 — heads a nine-coach rake on the 11.20 Waterloo to Exeter St David's service at Wimbledon on 19 August 2017.** *Alex Dasi- Sutton*

159107

159019

Gillingham
159101

159015

A contrast in liveries and typefaces for the running numbers sees South Western Railway-liveried No 159011 on the extreme right with Nos 159015 and 159018 in South West Trains livery, albeit now branded South Western Railway. The location is Basingstoke East Sidings and the date is 20 August 2018. *Gavin Morrison*

Opposite top: **It is 7 November 2017 and No 159102 heads a six-coach rake past the signal box at Gillingham with the 09.25 service from Exeter St David's to Waterloo. The BR-built box at Gillingham, which originally had a 30-lever frame, was abolished on 24 February 2012 in connection with the Basingstoke and West of England resignalling scheme. The box, at the time of writing, remains extant as it was retained to control the siding on the Up side and the associated shunt signals. For this purpose, five levers remain operational and are electronically released from Basingstoke.** *Alex Dasi-Sutton*

Bottom: **Over the years the skyline on the approaches to Vauxhall has changed radically and the traditional backdrop when recording Down services of the Palace of Westminster is rapidly disappearing behind trees and skyscrapers. On 22 June 2018 No 159015 leads a six-carriage rake towards the station with the 11.20 to Exeter St David's.** *Alex Dasi-Sutton*

On 22 August 2021 Nos 159012, the ill-fated victim of the collision on 31 October 2021, and 159015 head eastbound with the 13.25 service from Exeter St David's to Waterloo, recorded as it passes the signal box at Gillingham. *Alex Dasi-Sutton*

The last franchise livery that the class is likely to wear on the South Western main line is that of South Western Railway and it is in this livery that No 159003 is seen leading Nos 159016 and 158882 into Clapham Junction on 27 July 2023 with the 12.20 service from Waterloo to Exeter St David's. *Alex Dasi-Sutton*

Hythe Pier Railway

In operation now for more than a century, the railway that operates along Hythe Pier is now regarded as the pier railway that has operated continuously for the longest period.

The origins of the pier and its railway date back to at least the late 16th century when, in 1575, a ferry linking Hythe with Southampton was first recorded on a map produced by Christopher Saxton but it was not until the mid-19th century that any form of significant physical provision was made for vessels used on the service. In 1845 a stone pier — located slightly to the north of the present pier — was erected; known as the Hard, the facilities were primitive and, depending on the state of the tide, passengers often found themselves wading through water to and from the ferry. Moreover, as demand grew, the inadequacies of the Hard became greater. As a result, in 1870 a company was established to construct a new pier and, the following year, powers were sought for its construction. Hansard records on 5 May 1871 the minutes of a committee: 'Resolved, That the Chairman be directed to move the House, that leave be given to bring in a Bill to confirm certain Provisional Orders made by the Board of Trade under "The General Pier and Harbour Act, 1861," relating to Bournemouth, Carnlough, Clacton on Sea, Folkestone, Hythe (Southampton), and Withernsea.' The resultant Act received its Royal Assent on 13 July 1871.

The terminus at the Pier Head recorded on 12 April 1952. There is no run-round loop as the trains operate on the push-pull principle with a driver's cab at the seaward end of the leasing carriage. Clearly visible is the third rail used. *John Meredith/Online Transport Archive*

However, work did not commence and a new company — the Hythe Pier & Hythe & Southampton Ferry Co — was established in 1874 to take the project forward; the 1871 project was for a complex — and very expensive — structure that included a steam bridge landing pontoon. The plans envisaged for the 1874 scheme were much simpler (and cheaper). New powers were sought in parliament the following year and Hansard again reports on 7 April 1875: 'Resolved, That the Chairman be directed to move the House, that leave be given to bring in a Bill to confirm certain Provisional Orders made by the Board of Trade under "The General Pier and Harbour Act, 1861," relating to Coatham, Hythe (Southampton), Johnshaven, Newlyn, and Redcar.' The Pier and Harbour Confirmation (No 1) Act, which incorporated the Hythe Pier Order, received its Royal Assent on 13 May 1875. However, once again construction did not start, this time due to legal disagreements with the Southampton Harbour & Pier Board.

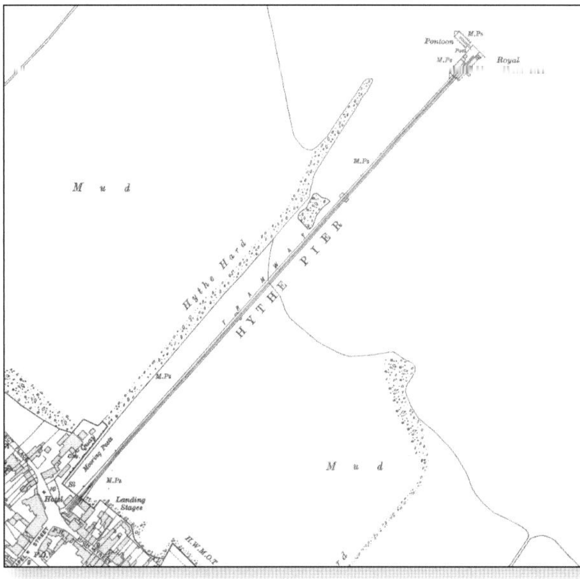

The pier and its tramway as recorded by the Ordnance Survey in 1932. *Reproduced with the permission of the National Library of Scotland*

A third attempt at constructing a new pier was launched two years later in November 1877. On 4 July 1878 the Royal Assent was given to the Pier and Harbour Orders Confirmation (No 1) Act, 1878. This covered the construction of a number of piers and other harbour facilities, including that at Hythe. With powers obtained, the process of fund raising commenced and, by July 1879, the requisite amount had been raised. The contract for the work — estimated at £7,700 — was let to Bergheim & Co of London (the same contractor who had constructed the pier at Bournemouth) who worked to a design produced by James Wright.

Work commenced on the construction of the pier in October 1879 and the last of the piles was driven in on 29 June 1880. Although the Act that the company had received for the construction of the pier included powers for the construction of a railway along the pier, this was not completed at this stage.

The landward terminus viewed on 31 August 1958 as one of the two operational tractors — No 1 — stands at the buffer stop. Adjacent to the tractor can be seen the luggage wagon; this was one of two acquired when the original narrow gauge line along the pier was opened in 1909. When the electric line was completed in 1922, one of the luggage wagons was regauged to operate on the new line. *John Meredith Collection/Online Transport Archive*

Viewed to the west on 29 April 1961 is the landward terminus. Apart from the platform road, the original facilities included two sidings, one of which provides access to the line's small shed. Visible in the centre is the small tanker that is used to supply fuel, as and when required, to the ferry in use. When the tanker was acquired is uncertain, but probably predates the Second World War. *John Meredith/Online Transport Archive*

In August 1964 MV *Hotspur II* is pictured moored on the pontoon at Hythe Pier awaiting departure for its next sailing across the Solent to Southampton. The ferry, with a gross tonnage of 54, was built by the Rowhedge Ironworks in Essex and entered service in 1936. Capable of carrying 300 passengers, the ferry was 56ft in length. Sold to the Clyde Marine Motoring Co in 1978 for use on the Gourock to Kilcreggan service and renamed *Kenilworth*, the 90-year-old vessel was withdrawn from regular service in 2007, having been re-engined in 2000, but retained for two years to provide morning and afternoon cruises. Subsequently sold, the ferry is at the time of writing undergoing restoration at Hartlepool. In late 2024 the pontoon was found to be damaged; this resulted in the suspension of the ferry service, which had still not been reinstated at the time of this article's preparation.
Geoffrey Tribe/Online Transport Archive

On the same day, a service heading back towards the landward terminus can be seen departing from the station at the Pier Head. Until 1963 the locomotives were painted in an all-over green livery and the rolling stock in green and cream; the transition to the new blue and white livery meant, however, that the older livery was still visible the following year. The two tractor units were originally fitted with full width windscreens but these were reduced in size shortly after their introduction to service. *Geoffrey Tribe/Online Transport Archive*

Bearing the blue and white livery adopted in the early 1960s, one of the tractor units and passenger coaches are seen at the Pier Head terminus on 5 June 1989. *Barry Cross*

The *Hampshire Advertiser* of 5 January 1881 described the completed structure: 'The pier is composed of a pair of longitudinal wrought iron open girders, resting upon groups of cast-iron screw piles, 40 feet apart, and well tied by diagonal and other braces, the girders themselves being held together with cross girders of nearly equal strength. The deck is formed of best pine joists, having the planks forming the floor, running in the direction of its length. The structure is singularly light, but possessing strength and rigidity far beyond any strains ever likely to be applied to it. The total length of the pier is a little over 2,100 feet, terminating in a spacious pier-head. The width of the pier proper is 16ft, the total surface being nearly 36,000 square feet.

'There are seven strong and very commodious landing stages, contiguous to the pier at different points along its length, so that everywhere passengers can land at all times of the tide. The stage at the pier head has, at the lowest state of the tide, a depth of 11ft. 6in. of water. Very neat wooden houses are erected at different points along the pier as shelter for those using it, and an elegant, commodious structure will shortly be erected upon the pier-head, embracing restaurant, waiting, music, and other rooms, for the use of the numerous visitors whom the beautiful promenade, the magnificent sea views, and charming scenery of the neighbourhood will attract.

'At the shore end it is proposed to retain about 400 feet of the existing hard, which will be raised above the sea level and converted into a quay for the landing of cattle and heavy merchandise.'

The pier finally opened on 1 January 1881. In order to move the luggage to and from the ferries, hand-operated trucks were utilised; however, these were found to be damaging the surface of the decking and, in 1909, they were replaced by a narrow gauge railway that was constructed on the north side of the pier. The construction was undertaken by E. J. Kingham, a Marchwood-based builder. The rolling stock — two luggage wagons — was again propelled by hand with the track being laid flush with the deck. The *Hampshire Independent* noted on 31 July 1909; 'the new tramway on the pier is now in use and luggage and goods are conveyed up and down on a couple of up-to-date trolleys.' On 12 February 1910 the same publication recorded: 'The tramway laid down on the pier for the conveyance of heavy goods and passengers' luggage has proved of great advantage and we notice that some additional sidings are now being put down by Mr. Kingham's workmen, which will greatly facilitate the traffic arrangements.' This system sufficed for more than a decade but it was in July 1922 that the new railway was opened, the engineer being Gerald Yorke.

By the late 1990s a new livery — predominantly white with red — had been adopted as evinced by a train standing in the platform at the landward end of the line on 30 July 1997. *Barry Cross*

One of the line's two surviving tractor units is seen at the landward terminus on 25 August 2005. Although numbers are carried, these are only shown on one side of cab — that on the other side from that viewed here. The cabs of the two tractors were modified in the 1970s with larger windscreens that were designed to increase driver's visibility. *Geoffrey Tribe/Online Transport Archive*

The new line was constructed on the south side. It was constructed to the 2ft 0in gauge and was electrified using a third rail; the latter was located on the south — sea side — of the track. The line itself is single track, with no passing loops, with two non-electrified sidings at the landward side. One of the latter is used to provide access to the line's workshop. Motive power was provided by three four-wheel locomotives that were constructed by Brush in 1917 for use at the mustard gas factory located at Avonmouth. Originally battery powered, these were converted to operate using the third rail at Hythe. Two of these locomotives — Works No 16302 and 16307 — remain with the line but the third — Works No 16304 — was broken up for spares in 1935. There are four passenger carriages; these were supplied by Drewry; two of them incorporate a driver's cab at the seaward end and the line is usually operated with the locomotive pushing the train outbound and hauling it on the return journey to the landward station. In addition, the line also possesses a four-wheel oil tanker, which is used when required to provide fuel for the ferry, and a four-wheel flat wagon for the conveyance of luggage (such as push chairs — unoccupied! — and other large items). As such the line can operate mixed passenger and freight trains and is probably the only place in the UK where a timetabled mixed train is operated at the present time.

The line has now operated for more than a century, albeit not without incident. The pier has been hit and damaged by vessels on a number of occasions. The earliest such event occurred on 30 July 1885 when five of the piles were damaged when the schooner *Annie* hit the pier. Thirty years later, on 26 August 1915, the pier was hit by the sailing barge *Itchen* although, on this occasion, the pier escaped unscathed. It was less fortunate in 1945 when it was hit and damaged by a landing craft. More serious damage occurred on 1 November 2003 when the pier was struck by the *Donald Redford*; the dredger destroyed a 46m section of the pier isolating the seaward terminus although, fortunately, there were no casualties. It was not until 7 January 2004 that the pier was fully restored. Most recently, the pier was hit by the ferry *Uriah Heep* on 13 May 2016, causing serious damage to the vessel. More positively, the railway has also been graced by the presence of royalty; it was on 24 May 1944 that King George VI visited the line although the commemorative brass work to mark the occasion has disappeared.

Right: **The interior of one of the four passenger carriages. Doors are only provided on one side of the coaches. The quartet are all bogie vehicles and, despite having Drewry maker's plates, were in fact constructed by Baguley Cars Ltd (Drewry was merely acting as the agent for the supply of the stock).**
Geoffrey Tribe/Online Transport Archive

Pictured at the Pier Head terminus on 25 August 2005, passengers make their way from the recently arrived train towards the pontoon and the ferry towards Southampton.
Geoffrey Tribe/Online Transport Archive

Between 1991 and 19 April 2017, when it was sold to Blue Funnel Cruises Ltd, the ferry service was operated by White Horse Ferries Ltd. On the same day in 2005 passengers are pictured disembarking from the MV *Great Expectations* at Southampton Town Quay. Built in 1992, the catamaran was originally designed for use on the ferry service between Gravesend and Tilbury, which was also operated by White Horse Ferries Ltd at the time, and was named after the Dickens novel that was set along the Thames. Transferred to the Solent in 1995. Following the sale of the ferry service in 2017 and a brief refit, the new owners renamed the ferry MV *Hythe Scene* on 26 May 2017 when it returned to service. The ferry remains operational although, at the time of writing, the service is suspended. *Geoffrey Tribe/Online Transport Archive*

Seaside piers are very vulnerable structures and, over the years, many have disappeared or been destroyed for a variety of reasons. The sad remains of the West Pier in Brighton are a vivid reminder of the loss of these fascinating structures. Fortunately, there is a group — the Hythe Pier Heritage Association (founded in 2018) — that has been actively involved in the conservation and preservation of the pier and its railway. Alongside work on the restoration and maintenance of the pier itself, much work has been completed over the past few years to ensure the survival of the railway. In 2020 and 2021 two of the four carriages were fully restored; at the time of writing work is being undertaken on the next. Out of service since 2019, one of the two tractor units was fully restored and formally named *Gerald Yorke* after the line's first engineer on 6 May 2021; the second tractor — No 2 — was taken out of service at the same time and was fully restored. It was completed and formally named *Edward Fort* on 14 June 2022. Also in 2022 work started on a programme of track replacement; this included work on the supporting wooden beams. The first 45m section at the landward end, which was completed in early 2024, also saw the construction of a new wooden station at this end of the line. This first phase of the line's restoration was officially opened by The Duke of Gloucester on 2 October 2024. In 2025 work commenced on the surviving luggage truck; this was one of the two that were produced in 1909 for the original narrow gauge railway but which had been regauged for use on the electric line in 1922.

Now operated by Red Funnel, the ferry service continues to provide a link between Hythe Pier and Town Quay; however, there were fears in late 2024 that the service might be scrapped when, following the discovery of damage to the pontoon at Hythe, the service was suspended on 22 August that year. With funding requests rejected by Hampshire County Council, Southampton City Council and New Forest District Council, the costs of repairing or replacing the pontoon — estimated at up to £250,000 — were problematic. However, it looks — at the time of writing — as though the link will be restored. Work commenced in May 2025 on the first stage of the repairs required. The ferry company was quoted by the *Daily Echo*: 'We're doing all we can to carefully manage timelines and budgets to get the ferry service up and running again as soon as possible, and in the most cost-effective way.' The company also confirmed that it was also committed to undertaking the ferry's annual refit (as required by the Maritime and Coastguard Agency).

SOUTHERN STATIONS 5
EAST HAMPSHIRE & WEST BERKSHIRE

Paul Smith

PLEASE NOTE THAT THE SCALES OF THE MAPS VARY AND ARE FOR ILLUSTRATIVE PURPOSES

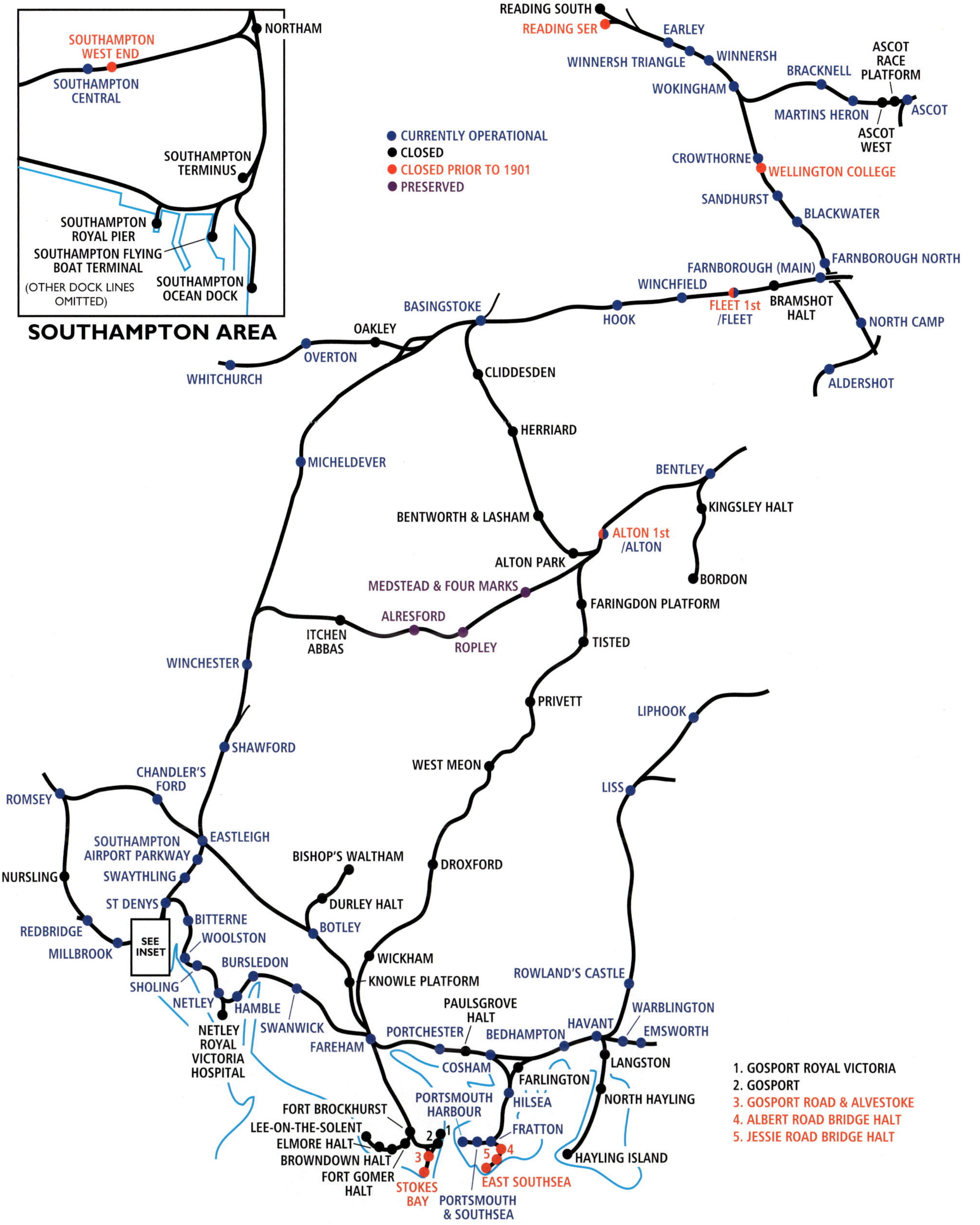

ALBERT ROAD BRIDGE HALT

Opened 1 July 1904 by the LB&SCR/L&SWR and closed 10 August 1914.

Line lifted – Demolished – Station site occupied by retail premises **SZ65600 98957**

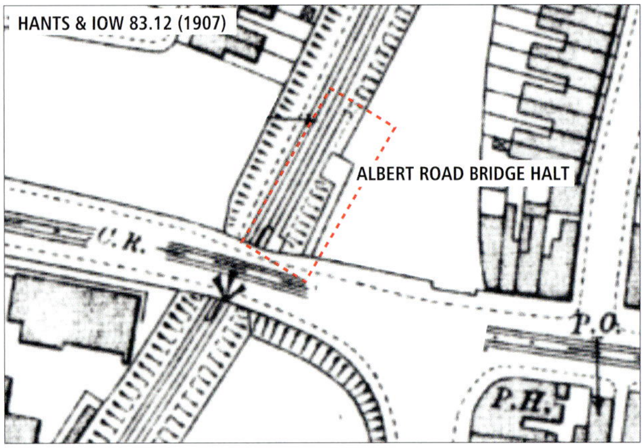

ALTON (1st)

Opened 28 July 1852 by the L&SWR and closed 2 October 1865.

Line lifted – Demolished – Station site partially in use as Alton Station Car Park **SU72374 39779 (a)**

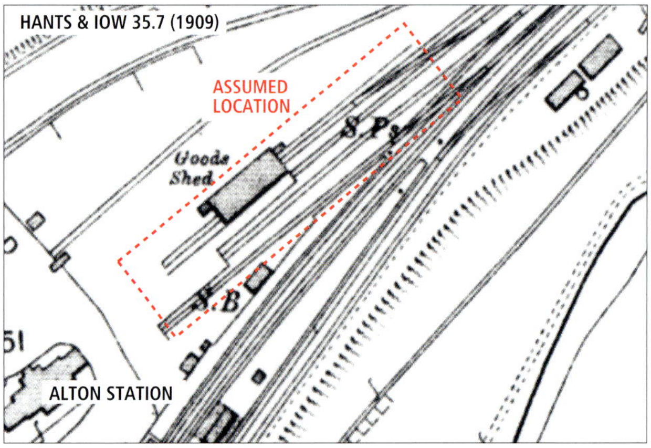

ALDERSHOT

Opened 2 May 1870 by the L&SWR as *Aldershot Town* and subsequently renamed as *Aldershot*.

SU86641 50421

Viewed on 16 April 2017

ALTON

Opened 2 October 1865 by the L&SWR as *Alton*, renamed as *Alton for Selborne* 5 July 1926 by the SR and reverted to *Alton* in 1955 by BR. *(Platforms 1 & 2). Shared with* **ALTON** [Mid-Hants Railway] *(Platform 3)*

SU72375 39727

Viewed on 14 April 2017

ALRESFORD

Opened 2 October 1865 by the Mid Hants Railway, closed 5 February 1973 by BR and reopened 30 April 1977 by the Mid-Hants Railway Preservation Society.

SU58799 32450

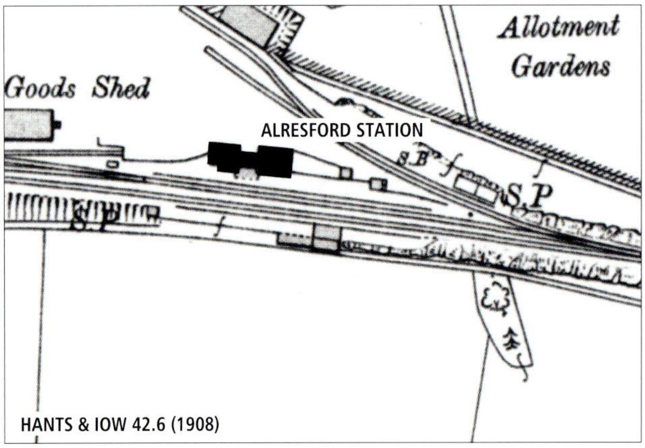

ALTON PARK

Opened in 1910 by the L&SWR and closed 11 September 1932 by the SR. (Also known as *Treloars Hospital Platform*)

Line lifted – Demolished – Station site unused within the grounds of Alton Community Hospital **SU70863 38401**

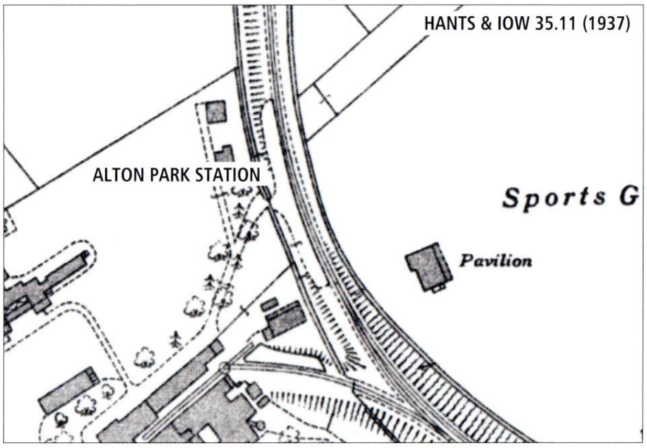

ASCOT

Opened 4 June 1856 by the Staines, Wokingham & Woking Junction Railway as *Ascot*, renamed as *Ascot & Sunninghill* 1 February 1857 and reverted to *Ascot* 10 July 1921 by the L&SWR. **SU92160 68297**

Viewed on 9 July 2017

ASCOT RACE PLATFORM

Opened 13 June 1911 by the L&SWR and closed c1975 by BR.

Line Operational – Demolished – No access

SU91795 68376

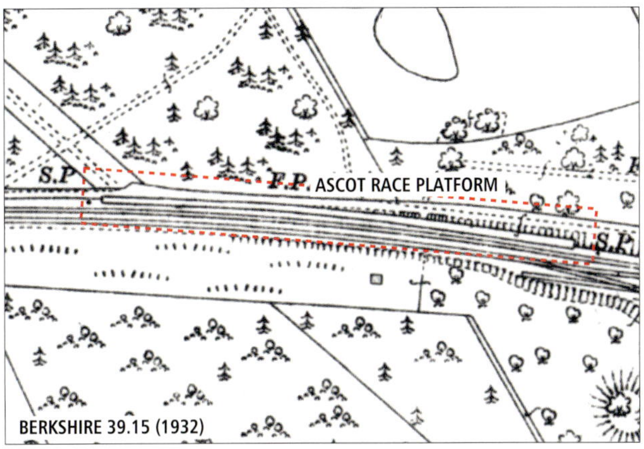

ASCOT WEST

Opened c1862 by the L&SWR and closed c1974 by BR.

Line Operational – Demolished – No access

SU90574 68311

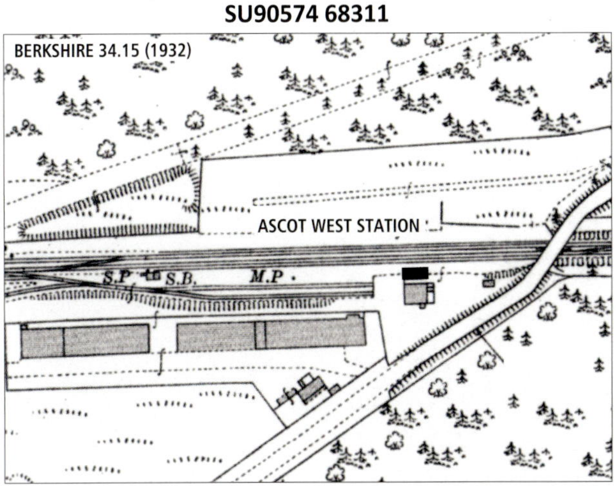

BASINGSTOKE

Opened 10 June 1839 by the L&SWR as *Basingstoke* renamed as *Basingstoke Junction* in 1854 and reverted to *Basingstoke* in c1859.

SU63799 52575

Viewed on 9 July 2017

BEDHAMPTON

Opened 1 April 1906 by the LB&SCR as *Bedhampton Halt* and renamed as *Bedhampton* 5 May 1969 by BR.

SU70760 06538

Viewed on 14 April 2017

BENTLEY

Opened prior to July 1854 by the L&SWR.

SU79201 43054

Viewed on 14 April 2017

BENTWORTH & LASHAM

Opened 1 June 1901 by the Basingstoke & Alton Light Railway, closed 1 January 1917 by the L&SWR, reopened 18 August 1924 by the SR and finally closed 12 September 1932.

Line lifted – Demolished – Station site in commercial use
SU66922 41719

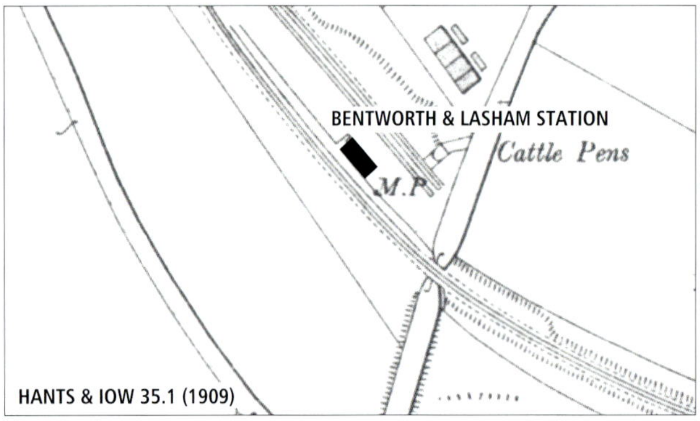

HANTS & IOW 35.1 (1909)

BISHOP'S WALTHAM

Opened 1 June 1863 by the Bishop's Waltham Railway and closed 1 January 1933 by the SR.

Line lifted – Demolished – Station site occupied by "The Old Station Roundabout" **SU55025 17504**

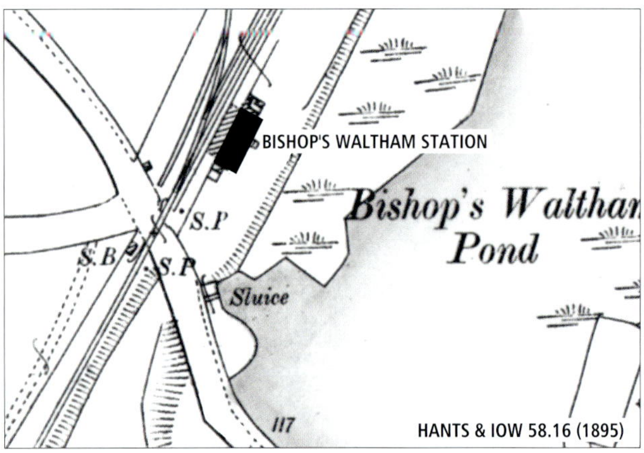

HANTS & IOW 58.16 (1895)

BITTERNE

Opened 5 March 1866 by the Southampton & Notley Railway as *Bitterne Road* and renamed as *Bitterne* 20 September 1896. **SU43877 13397**

Viewed on 3 October 2015

BLACKWATER

Opened 4 July 1849 by the Reading, Guildford & Reigate Railway as *Blackwater*, renamed as *Blackwater and Sandhurst* in August 1851 by the SER, as *Blackwater* in June 1852, as *Blackwater and York Town* in May 1897 by the SE&CR, as *Blackwater and Camberley* 9 July 1923 by the SR and as *Blackwater* by BR.

SU85298 59897

Viewed on 16 April 2017

BORDON

Opened 11 December 1905 by the L&SWR and closed 16 September 1957 by BR.

Line lifted – Demolished – Station site occupied by "Bordon Trading Estate" **SU78335 36232**

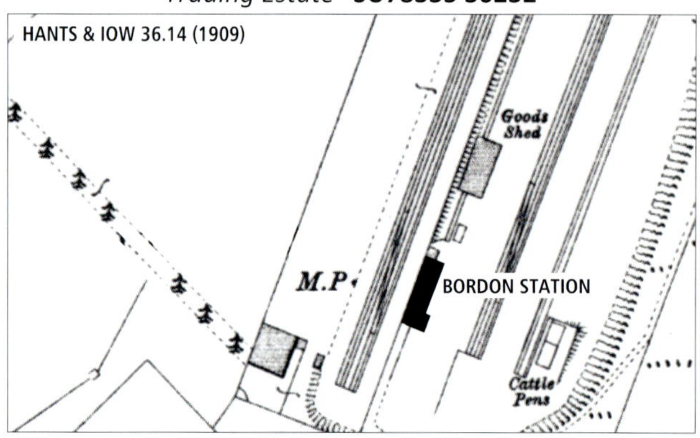

HANTS & IOW 36.14 (1909)

BOTLEY

Opened 29 November 1841 by the LB&SCR, closed 2 December 1841, reopened 7 February 1842, renamed as *Botley Halt* 14 July 1968 by BR and as *Botley* 5 May 1969.

SU52156 13271

Viewed on 2 October 2015

BRACKNELL

Opened 9 July 1856 by the Staines, Woking & Wokingham Junction Railway.

SU86841 68964

Viewed on 9 July 2017

BRAMSHOT HALT

Opened 10 May 1913 by the L&SWR and closed 6 May 1946 by the SR.

Line Operational – Demolished – No access

SU83032 38250

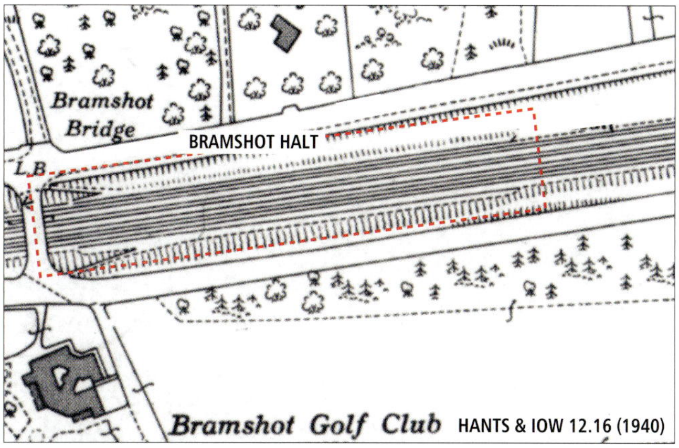

HANTS & IOW 12.16 (1940)

BROWNDOWN HALT

Opened 12 May 1894 by the Lee-on-the-Solent Railway closed 31 August 1914 by the L&SWR, reopened 1 October 1914 and closed 1 May 1930 by the SR.

Line lifted – Demolished – Station site unused on MOD property **SZ57803 99482**

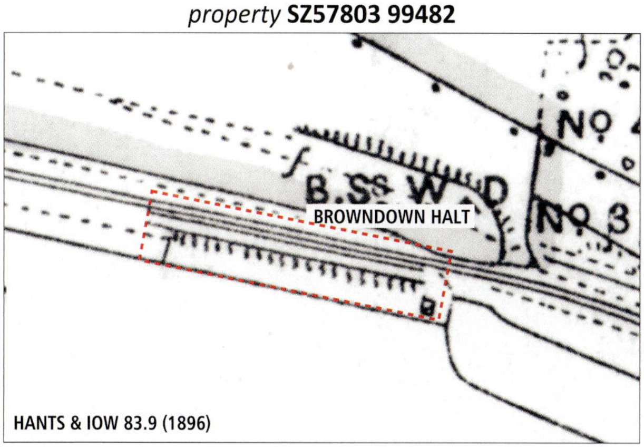

HANTS & IOW 83.9 (1896)

BURSLEDON

Opened 2 September 1899 by the L&SWR.

SU48996 09605

Viewed on 14 April 2017

CHANDLERS FORD

Opened 1 March 1847 by the L&SWR, closed 5 May 1969 by BR and reopened 18 May 2003.

SU43274 20633

Viewed on 3 October 2015

CLIDDESDEN

Opened 1 June 1901 by the Basingstoke & Alton Light Railway, closed 1 January 1917 by the L&SWR, reopened 18 August 1924 by the SR and finally closed 12 September 1932.

Line lifted – Demolished – Station site in private use (Oh Mr Porter! was filmed here in 1937) **SU63816 49060**

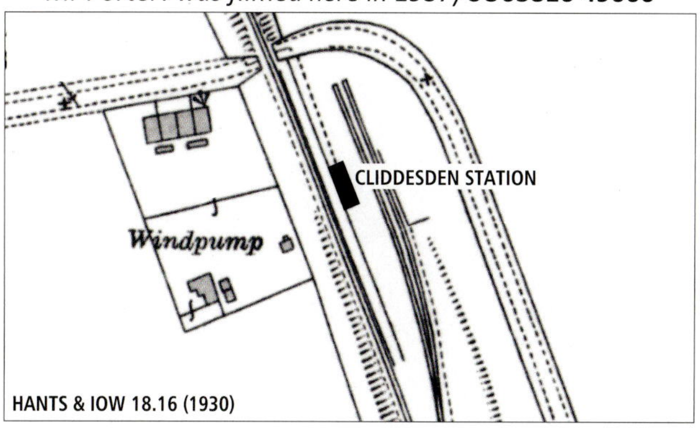

HANTS & IOW 18.16 (1930)

COSHAM

Opened 1 September 1848 by the L&SWR.
SU65784 05118

Viewed on 14 April 2017

CROWTHORNE

Opened by the SER in c1860 as *Wellington College* renamed as *Wellington College for Crowthorne* in c1895 and as *Crowthorne* 17 June 1928 by the SR.
SU82296 63707

Viewed on 16 April 2017

DROXFORD

Opened 1 June 1903 by the L&SWR and closed 7 February 1955 by BR.
Line lifted - Station building, canopy and platform in private use **SU61243 18562**

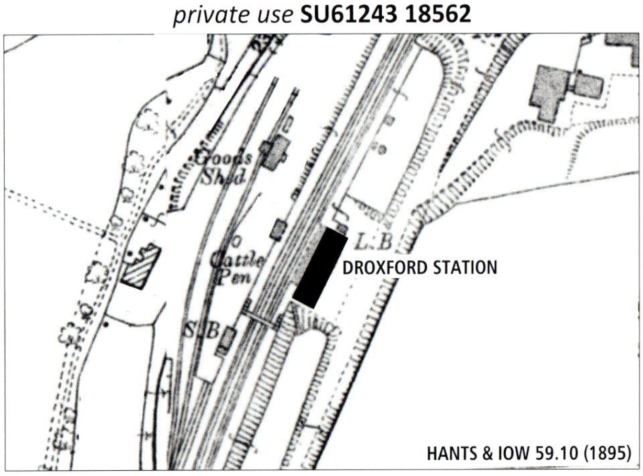

HANTS & IOW 59.10 (1895)

DURLEY HALT

Opened 23 December 1909 by the L&SWR and closed 1 January 1933 by the SR.
Line lifted – Demolished - Degraded platform partially extant – Station site unused **SU52534 15050**

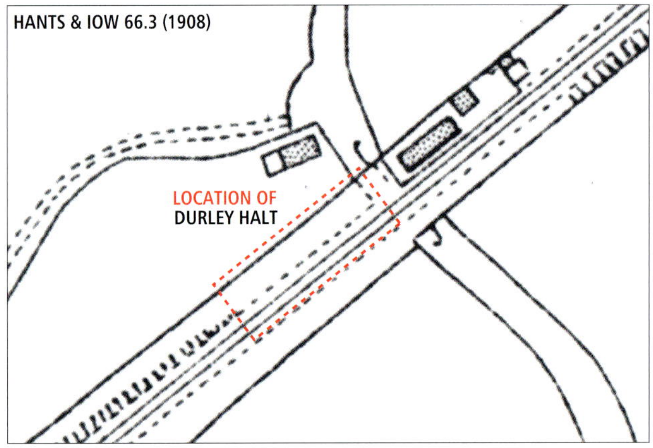

HANTS & IOW 66.3 (1908)

EARLEY

Opened 1 November 1863 by the SER.
SU75310 71892

Viewed on 16 April 2017

EASTLEIGH

Opened 29 November 1841 by the L&SWR as *Bishopstoke* renamed as *Eastleigh & Bishopstoke* in 1889, as *Eastleigh for Bishopstoke* 9 July 1923 by the SR and as *Eastleigh* in 1955 by BR. **SU45746 19038**

Viewed on 1 December 2012

EAST SOUTHSEA

Opened 2 July 1885 by the Southsea Railway as *Southsea* renamed as *East Southsea* in 1896 by the L&SWR/LB&SCR and closed 8 August 1914.

Line lifted – Demolished – Chewter Close crosses the station site **SZ65007 98380**

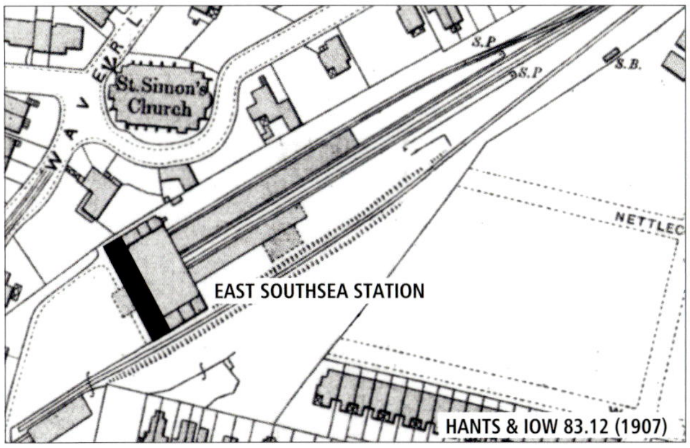

HANTS & IOW 83.12 (1907)

ELMORE HALT

Opened 11 April 1910 by the L&SWR, closed 31 August 1914, reopened 1 October 1914 and finally closed 1 May 1930 by the SR.

Line lifted – Demolished – Station site occupied by parking area for boats for the "Lee-on-the-Solent Sailing Club"

SZ56728 99741

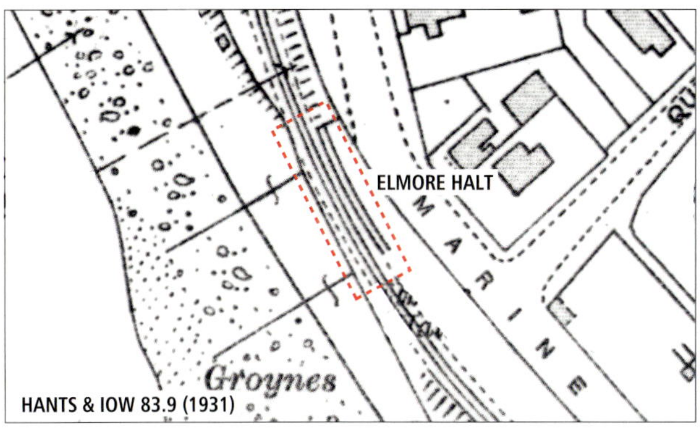

HANTS & IOW 83.9 (1931)

EMSWORTH

Opened 15 March 1847 by the Brighton & Chichester Railway **SU74760 06331**

Viewed on 1 October 2016

FAREHAM

Opened 29 November 1841 by the L&SWR as *Fareham Junction* and renamed as *Fareham* in 1853.

SU56946 06308

Viewed on 14 April 2017

FARINGDON PLATFORM

Opened 15 May 1931 by the SR as *Faringdon Platform* renamed as *Farringdon* 8 July 1934 and closed 7 February 1955 by BR.

Line lifted – Demolished – Station site occupied by the "Faringdon Industrial Centre" **SU70411 34936**

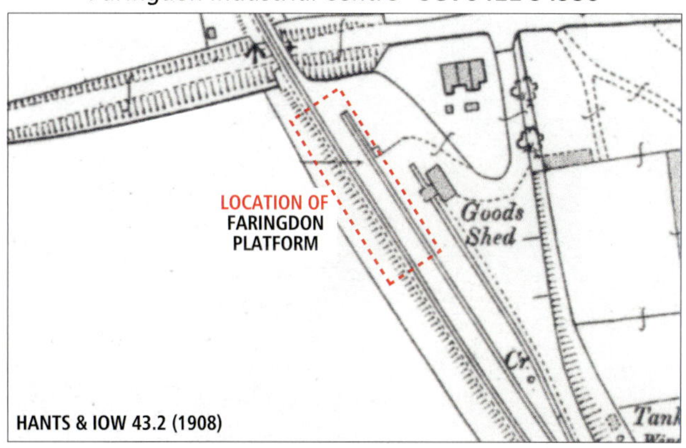

HANTS & IOW 43.2 (1908)

FARLINGTON HALT

Opened 26 June 1891 by the LB&SCR as *Farlington Race Station*, closed in 1922, reopened in 1922, closed in 1927 by the SR, reopened 17 June 1928 as *Farlington Halt* and finally closed 4 July 1937.

Line Operational – Demolished – No access

SU67259 04705

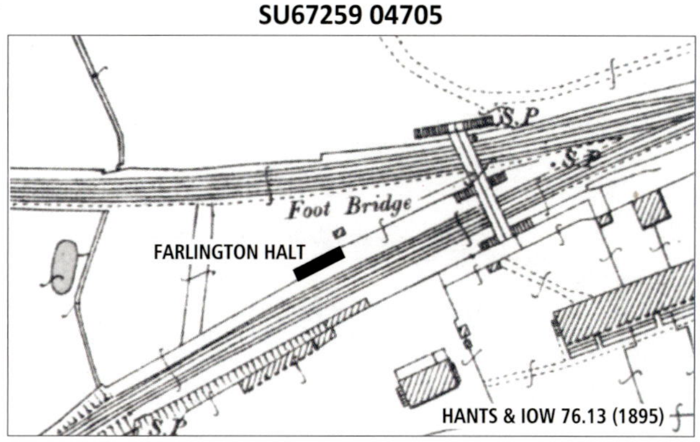

HANTS & IOW 76.13 (1895)

FARNBOROUGH (MAIN)

Opened 24 September 1838 by the London & Southampton Railway as *Farnborough* and renamed as *Farnborough (Main)* 12 May 1980 by BR.

SU86853 56035

FARNBOROUGH NORTH

Opened 4 July 1849 by the Reading, Guildford & Reigate Railway as *Farnborough* and renamed as *Farnborough North* 9 July 1923 by the SR.

SU87729 56655

FLEET (1st)

Opened in February 1848 by the L&SWR as *Fleetpond* renamed as *Fleet* 1 July 1869 and closed in 1904.

Line Operational – Demolished – No access

SU81413 55239

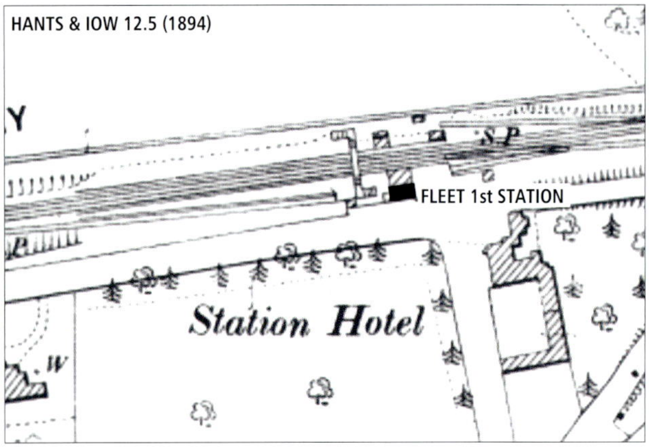

FLEET

Opened in 1904 by the L&SWR

SU81628 55269

FORT BROCKHURST

Opened in 1865 by the Stokes Bay Railway & Pier as *Brockhurst*, renamed as *Fort Brockhurst* 23 November 1893 by the L&SWR and closed 8 June 1953 by BR.

Line lifted - Station building and platforms in private use

SU59509 01250

FORT BROCKHURST (Lee-on-the-Solent Railway)

Opened 12 May 1894 by the Lee-on-the-Solent Railway and closed 31 December 1930 by the SR.

Line lifted - Station building and platforms in private use

SU59527 01193

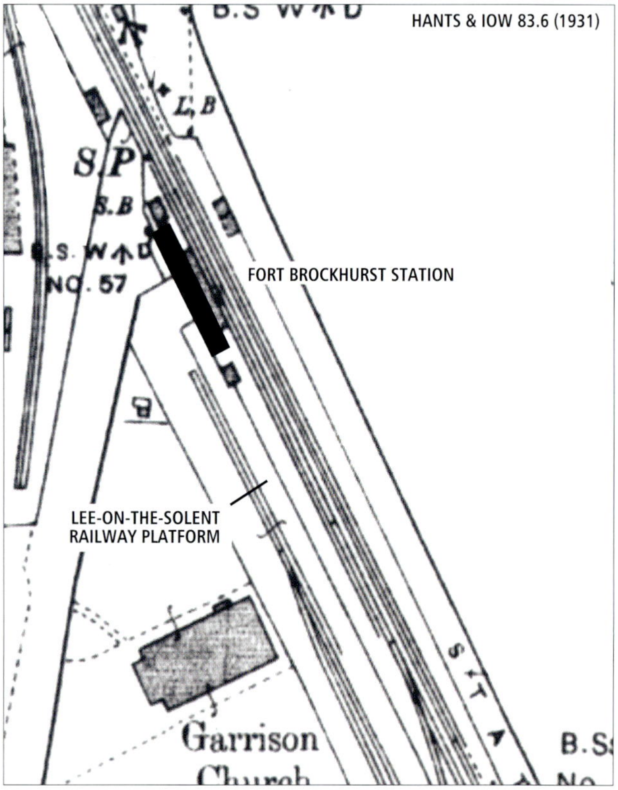

FORT GOMER HALT

Opened 12 May 1894 by the Lee-on-the-Solent Railway as *Privett*, renamed as *Fort Gomer* in 1909 by the L&SWR, as *Fort Gomer Halt* in 1910, closed 31 August 1914, reopened 1 October 1914 and finally closed 1 May 1930 by the SR.

Line lifted – Demolished – The B333, Privett Road, passes through the station site **SZ59041 99754**

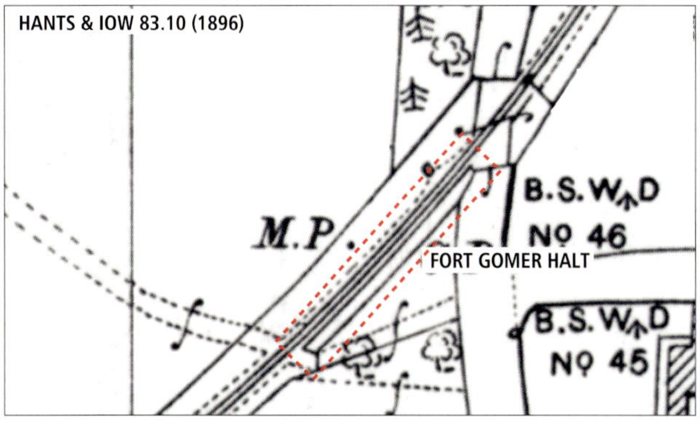

FRATTON

Opened 2 July 1885 by the L&SWR/LB&SCR as *Fratton* renamed as *Fratton & Southsea* 4 July 1905 and reverted to *Fratton* 1 December 1921.

SU65408 00062

Viewed on 15 April 2017

GOSPORT

Opened 29 November 1841 by the L&SWR and closed 8 June 1953 by BR.

Line lifted - Station building restored and in residential and commercial use **SU61397 00188**

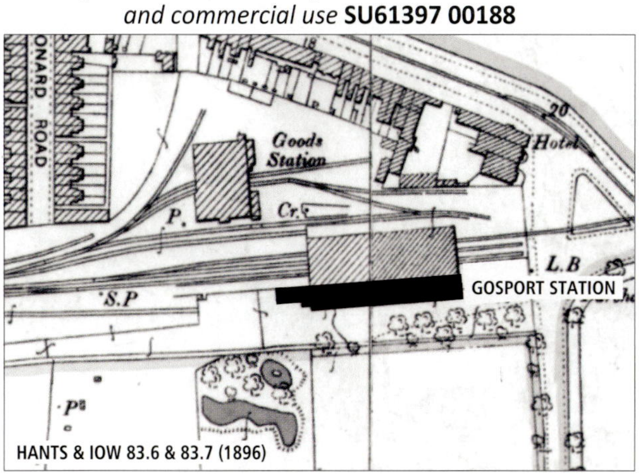

GOSPORT ROAD & ALVERSTOKE

Opened 1 June 1865 by the Stokes Bay Railway & Pier as *Stoke Road*, renamed as *Gosport Road* 8 November 1866 as *Gosport Road & Alverstoke* in 1893 by the L&SWR and closed 1 November 1915.

Line lifted – Demolished – Station site occupied by BT telephone exchange building **SZ60761 99516**

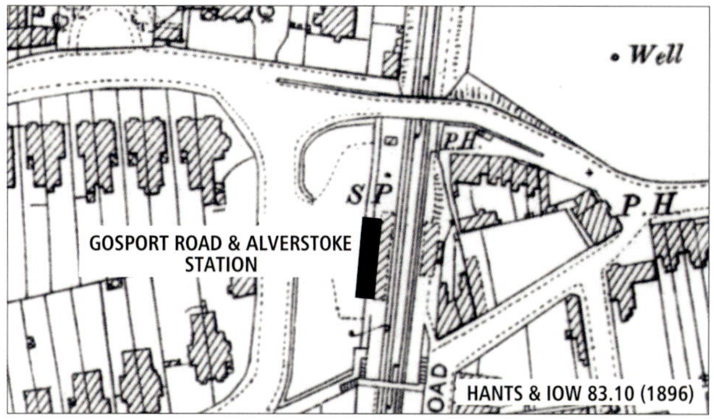

GOSPORT ROYAL VICTORIA

Opened 13 September 1845 by the L&SWR and closed 2 December 1901.

Line lifted – Demolished – Station site in commercial use

SU61826 00474

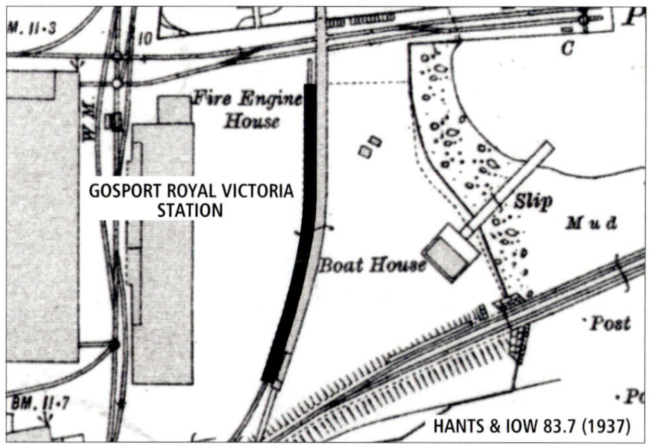

HAMBLE

Opened 18 January 1942 by the SR as *Hamble Halt* and renamed as *Hamble* 15 May 1969 by BR.

SU47321 08189

Viewed on 3 October 2015

HAVANT

Opened 15 March 1847 by the Brighton & Chichester Railway. **SU71784 06602**

HAYLING ISLAND

Opened 15 July 1867 by the Hayling Railway as *Hayling Island*, closed in December 1868, reopened in August 1869 as *South Hayling*, reverted to *Hayling Island* 1 June 1892 by the LB&SCR and closed 4 November 1963 by BR.

Line lifted – Demolished – Station site occupied by a car park – The Hayling Billy Leisure Trail commences at the station site **SZ70936 99793**

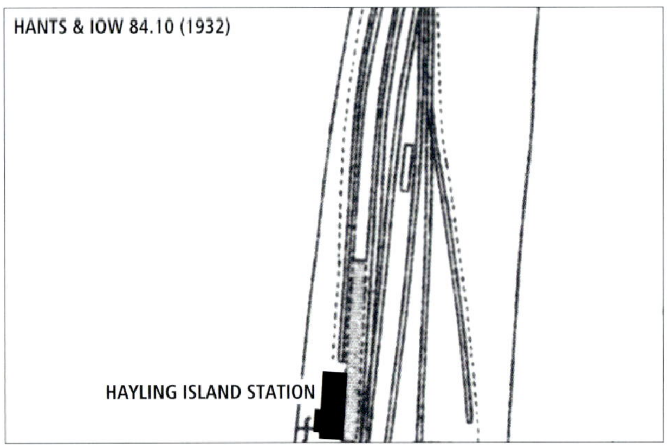

HERRIARD

Opened 1 June 1901 by the Basingstoke & Alton Light Railway, closed 1 January 1917 by the L&SWR, reopened 18 August 1924 by the SR and closed 12 September 1932.

Line lifted – Demolished – Station site in private use **SU66737 45054**

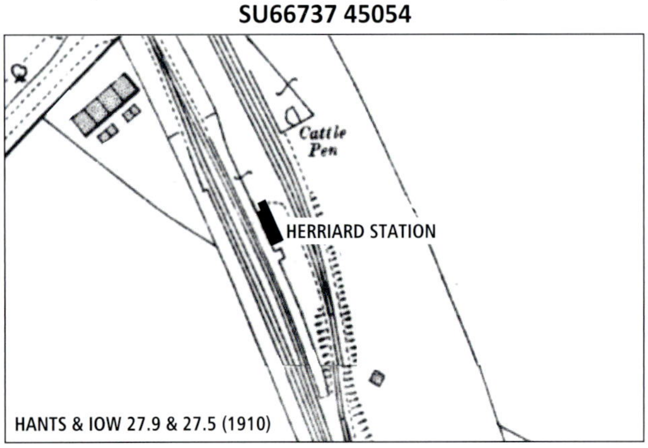

HILSEA

Opened 2 November 1941 by the SR as *Hilsea Halt* and renamed as *Hilsea* 5 May 1969 by BR. **SU66379 03607**

HOOK

Opened 2 July 1883 by the L&SWR. **SU72541 53931**

ITCHEN ABBAS

Opened 2 October 1865 by the Mid Hants Railway and closed 5 February 1973 by BR.

Line lifted – Demolished – Station site occupied by a dwelling **SU53216 33037**

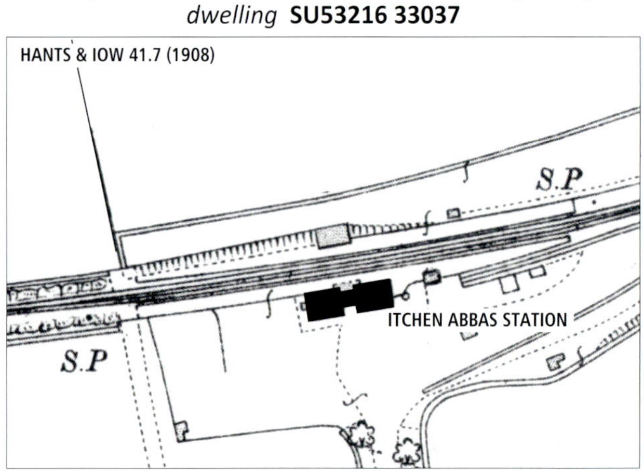

JESSIE ROAD BRIDGE HALT

Opened 1 July 1904 by the LB&SCR/L&SWR and closed 10 August 1914.

Line lifted - Demolished – A short driveway passes through the station site **SZ65736 99533**

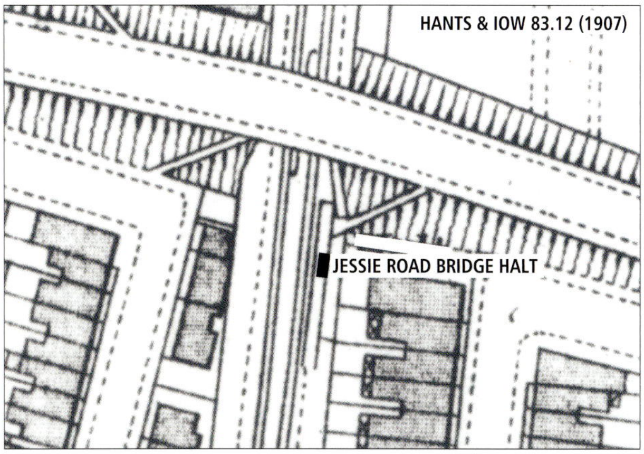

LANGSTON

Opened 15 July 1867 by the Hayling Railway as *Langstone* closed in December 1868, reopened in August 1869 renamed as *Langston* in May 1875 by the LB&SCR and closed 4 November 1963 by BR.

Line lifted – Demolished – Station site in private use **SU71652 05047**

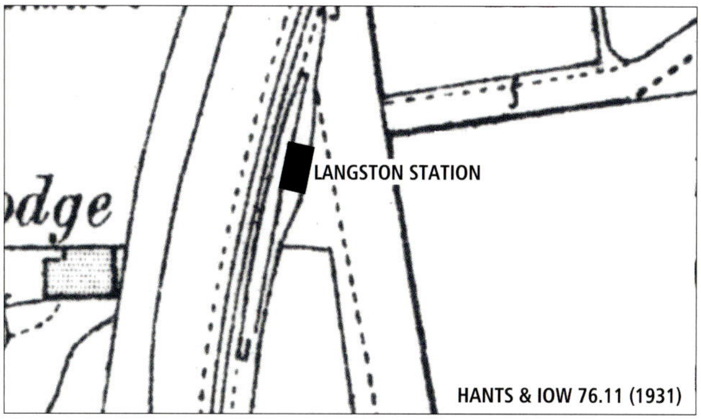

KINGSLEY HALT

Opened 7 March 1906 by the L&SWR and closed 16 September 1957.

Line lifted – Demolished – Station site unused **SU78789 39066**

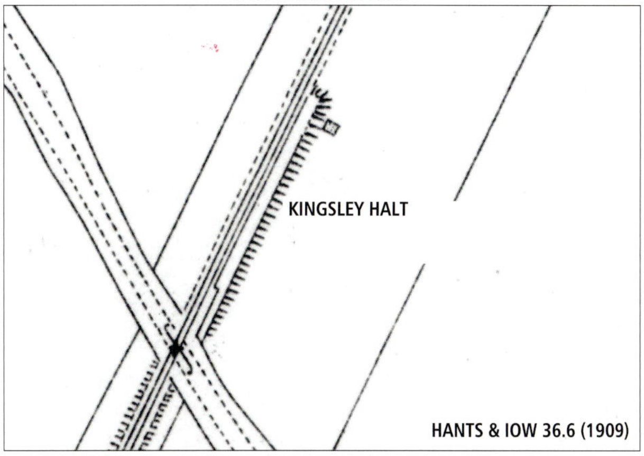

LEE-ON-THE-SOLENT

Opened 12 May 1894 by the Lee-on-the-Solent Railway closed 31 August 1914 by the L&SWR, reopened 1 October 1914 and finally closed 1 January 1931 by the SR.

Line lifted - Station building in private use as an amusement arcade – Remainder of station site occupied by a picnic area **SU56247 00444**

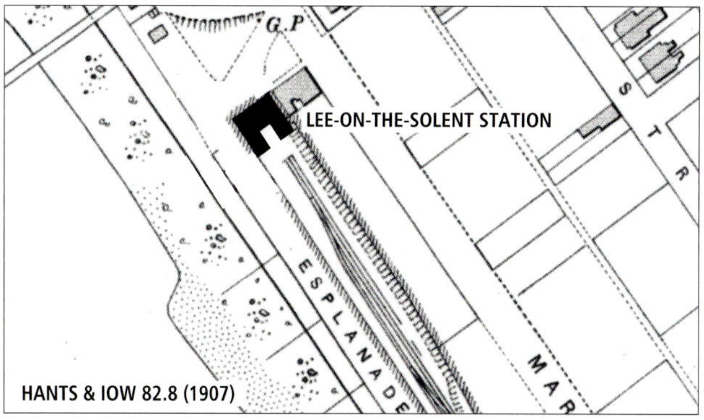

KNOWLE PLATFORM

Opened 1 May 1907 by the L&SWR as *Knowle Asylum Halt* renamed as *Knowle Platform* 2 June 1907, as *Knowle Halt* 5 October 1942 by the SR and closed 6 April 1964 by BR.

Line Operational - Demolished – Platforms partially extant – No access **SU55819 09471**

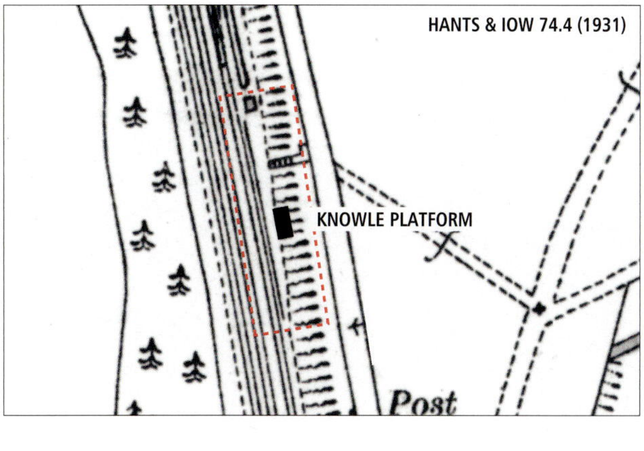

LIPHOOK

Opened 1 January 1859 by the Portsmouth Railway.

SU84165 30902

LISS

Opened 1 January 1859 by the Portsmouth Railway.

SU77717 27744

Viewed on 14 April 2017

MARTINS HERON

Opened 3 October 1988.

SU88763 68392

Viewed on 9 July 2017

MEDSTEAD & FOUR MARKS

Opened 1 August 1868 by the Mid Hants Railway as *Medstead*, renamed as *Medstead & Four Marks* 1 October 1937 by the SR, closed 5 February 1973 by BR and reopened 25 May 1985 by the Mid Hants Railway Preservation Society.

SU66850 35314

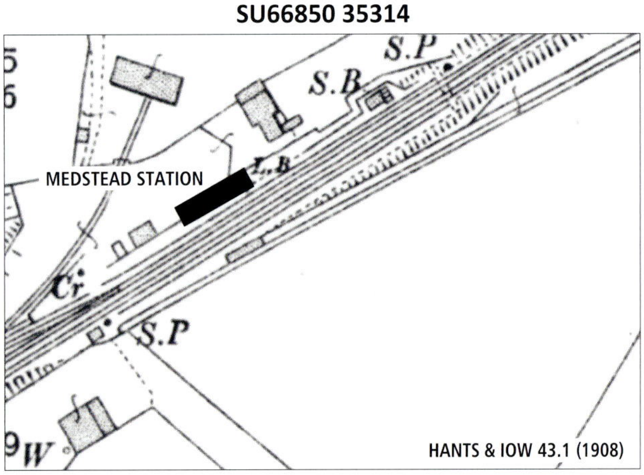

MICHELDEVER

Opened 11 May 1840 by the L&SWR as *Andover Road* and renamed as *Micheldever* in 1856.

SU51789 42848

Viewed on 22 September 2016

MILLBROOK (Hants)

Opened 1 November 1861 by the L&SWR as *Millbrook* and renamed as *Millbrook (Hants)* 12 May 1980.

SU39909 12596

Viewed on 3 October 2015

NETLEY

Opened 5 March 1866 by the L&SWR.

SU46408 08595

Viewed on 3 October 2015

NETLEY ROYAL VICTORIA HOSPITAL

Opened 18 April 1900 by the L&SWR and closed c1945 by the SR.

Line lifted – Demolished – Station site landscaped as part of the "Royal Victoria Country Park" – The Hamble Rail Trail passes through the station site **SU46572 07621**

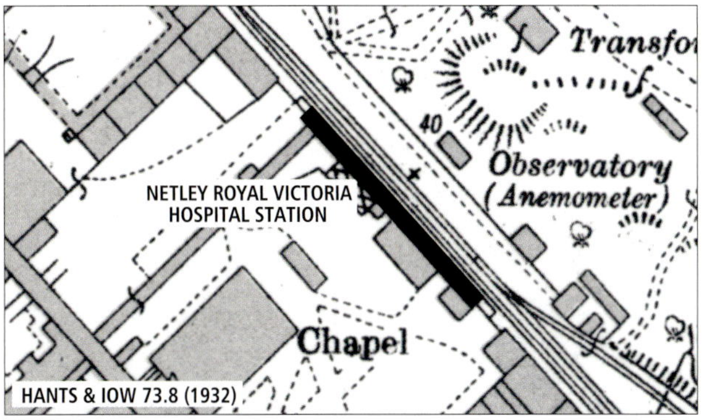

HANTS & IOW 73.8 (1932)

NORTH HAYLING

Opened 15 July 1867 by the Hayling Railway, closed in December 1868, reopened in August 1869 and closed 4 November 1963 by BR

Line lifted – Demolished – The Hayling Billy Leisure Trail passes through the station site **SU71724 02974**

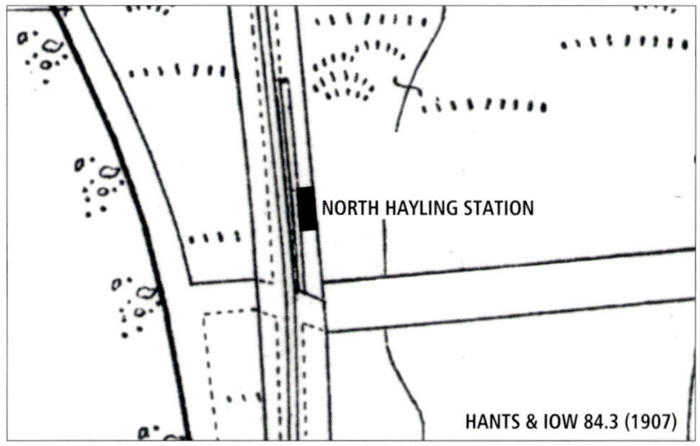

HANTS & IOW 84.3 (1907)

NORTHAM

Opened 1 December 1872 by the L&SWR and closed 5 September 1966 by BR.

Line Operational – Demolished - No access

SU42820 12218

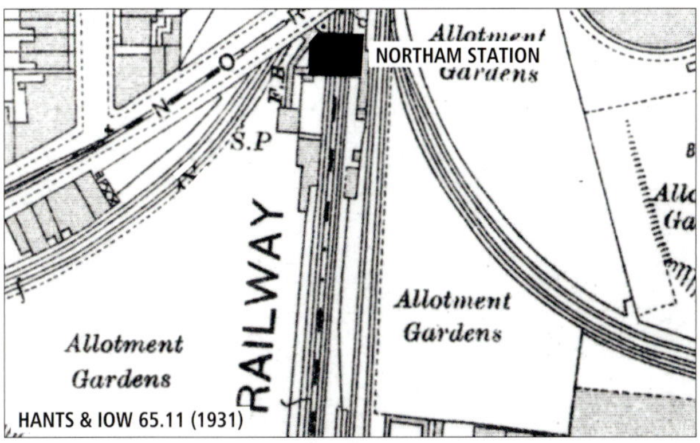

HANTS & IOW 65.11 (1931)

NURSLING

Opened 19 November 1883 by the L&SWR and closed 16 September 1957 by BR.

Line Operational - Station House in private use – Platforms demolished **SU36389 16047**

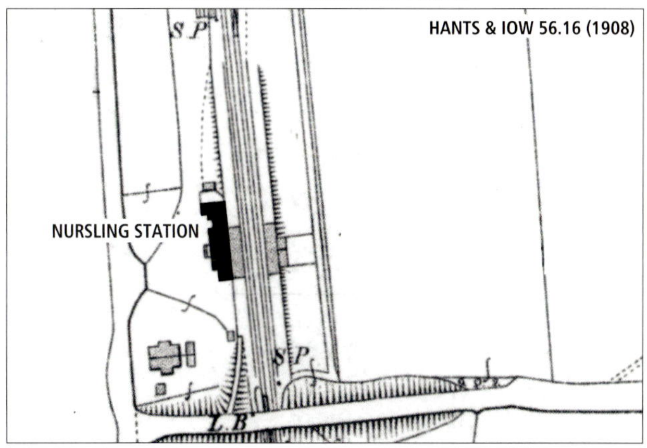

HANTS & IOW 56.16 (1908)

NORTH CAMP

Opened in August 1857 by the SER as *North Camp Aldershot*, renamed as *Aldershot Camp* in June 1863, as *Aldershot (North Camp)* 1 May 1879, as *Aldershot (North Camp) & South Farnborough* 1 May 1909 by the SE&CR, as *Aldershot North* 9 July 1923 by the SR and as *North Camp* 13 June 1955 by BR.

SU88621 53715

Viewed on 16 April 2017

OAKLEY

Opened 10 March 1856 by the L&SWR and closed 17 June 1963 by BR.

Line Operational – Station building and site in commercial use **SU56763 50962**

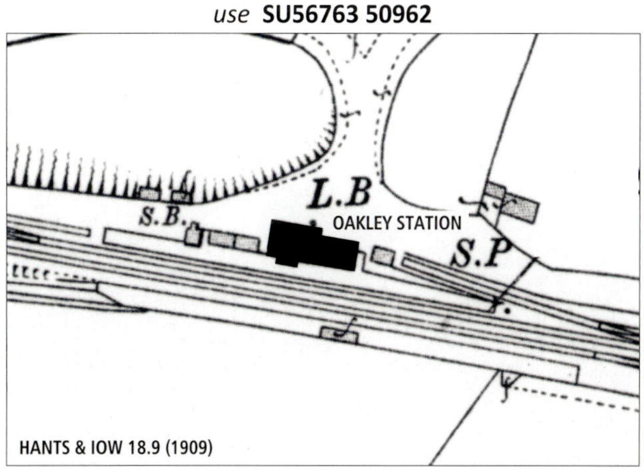

HANTS & IOW 18.9 (1909)

OVERTON

Opened 1 December 1854 by the L&SWR.

SU51737 50812

Viewed on 22 September 2016

PAULSGROVE HALT

Opened 28 June 1933 by the SR and closed in 1957 by BR.

Line Operational – Demolished – No access

SU63730 05766

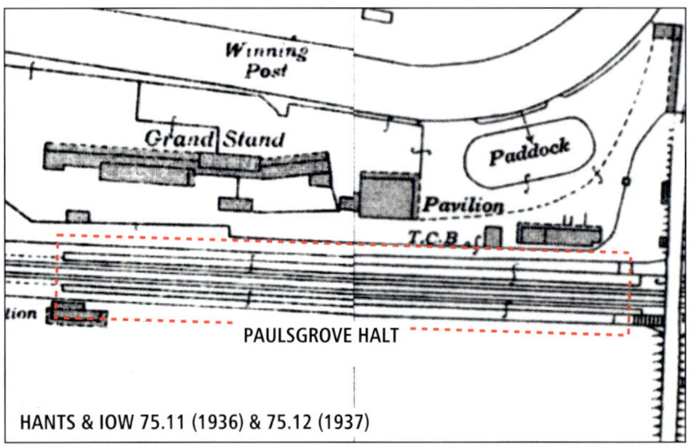

HANTS & IOW 75.11 (1936) & 75.12 (1937)

PORTCHESTER

Opened 1 September 1848 by the L&SWR.

SU61693 05847

Viewed on 14 April 2017

PORTSMOUTH & SOUTHSEA

Opened 14 June 1847 by the LB&SCR/L&SWR as *Portsmouth*, renamed as *Portsmouth Town* 2 October 1876 and as *Portsmouth & Southsea* 1 December 1921.

SU64221 00254

Viewed on 15 April 2017

PORTSMOUTH HARBOUR

Opened 2 October 1876 by the LB&SCR/L&SWR.

SU62935 00079

Viewed on 15 April 2017

PRIVETT

Opened 1 June 1903 by the L&SWR and closed 7 February 1955 by BR.

Line lifted – Station building in private use

SU67339 28639

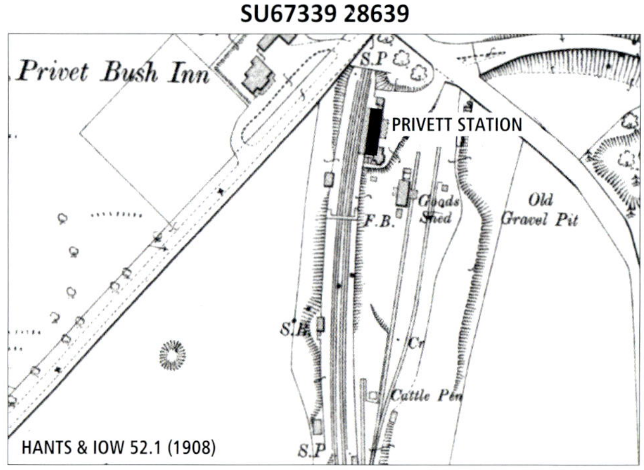

HANTS & IOW 52.1 (1908)

READING

Opened 4 July 1849 by the Reading, Guildford & Reigate Railway and closed 30 August 1855 by the SER.

Line lifted – Demolished – Forbury Road crosses over the west end of the station site, remainder in commercial use

SU71816 73714 (a)

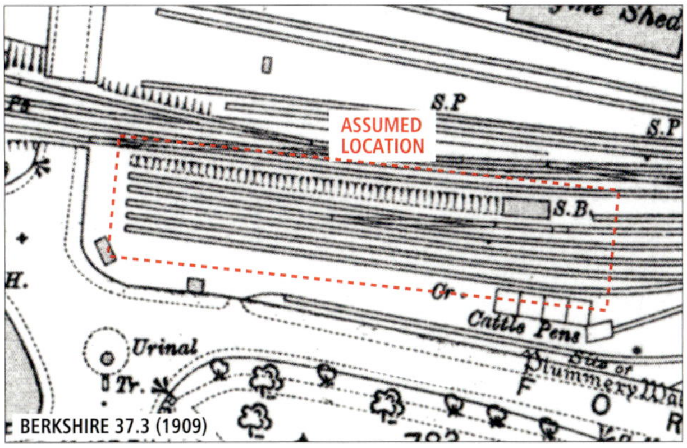

ROMSEY

Opened 1 March 1847 by the L&SWR.

SU35639 21614

READING SOUTH

Opened 30 August 1855 by the SER as *Reading*, renamed as *Reading South* 26 September 1949 by BR, as *Reading Southern* 11 September 1961 and closed 6 September 1965.

Line lifted – Demolished - Station site occupied by an office block **SU71595 73760**

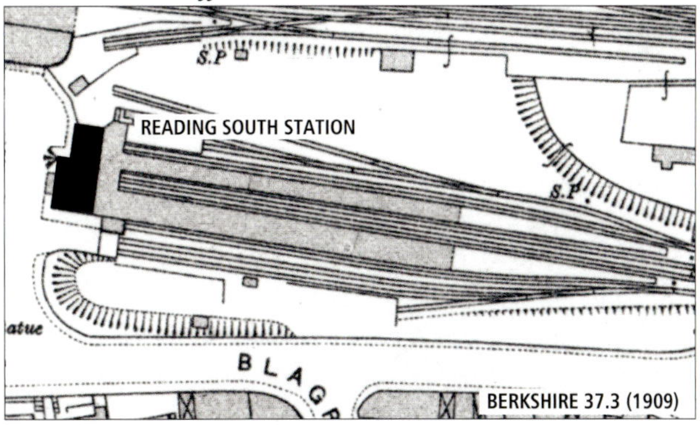

ROPLEY

Opened 2 October 1865 by the Mid Hants Railway, closed 5 February 1973 by BR and reopened 30 April 1977 by the Mid Hants Railway Preservation Society.

SU62951 32400

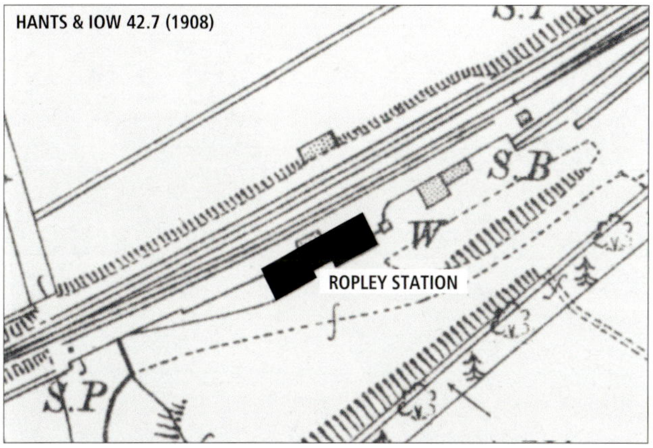

REDBRIDGE

Opened 1 June 1847 by the L&SWR.

SU37313 13513

ROWLANDS CASTLE

Opened 1 January 1859 by the Portsmouth Railway.

SU73419 10806

ST DENYS

Opened 5 March 1866 by the L&SWR as Portswood and renamed as St Denys 1 January 1876.

SU43134 13852

Viewed on 3 October 2015

SHOLING

Opened 1 August 1866 by the L&SWR.

SU44784 10985

Viewed on 3 October 2015

SANDHURST

Opened 4 May 1852 by the SER as *Sandhurst Halt*, closed 31 December 1853, reopened in August 1909 by the SE&CR and renamed as *Sandhurst* 5 May 1969 by BR.

SU83396 61516

Viewed on 16 April 2017

SOUTHAMPTON AIRPORT (PARKWAY)

Opened 1 April 1966 by BR as *Southampton Airport* renamed as *Southampton Parkway* 29 September 1986 and as *Southampton Airport (Parkway)* 29 May 1994 by Railtrack. **SU44841 16994**

Viewed on 3 October 2015

SHAWFORD

Opened 1 September 1882 by the L&SWR as *Shawford & Twyford*, renamed as *Shawford for Twyford* in 1923 by the SR and as *Shawford* in 1955 by BR.

SU47250 24970

Viewed on 3 October 2015

SOUTHAMPTON CENTRAL

Opened 1 November 1895 by the L&SWR as *Southampton West*, renamed as *Southampton Central* 7 July 1935 by the SR, as *Southampton* 10 July 1967 by BR and reverted to *Southampton Central* 19 April 1994 by Railtrack.

SU41292 12168

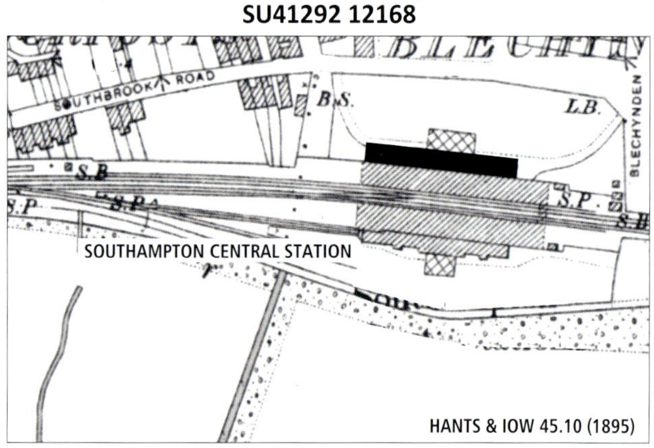

HANTS & IOW 45.10 (1895)

SOUTHAMPTON FLYING BOAT TERMINAL

Opened 14 April 1948 by BR and closed in September 1958.

Line lifted – Demolished - Station site occupied by part of a vehicle park **SU42095 10732**

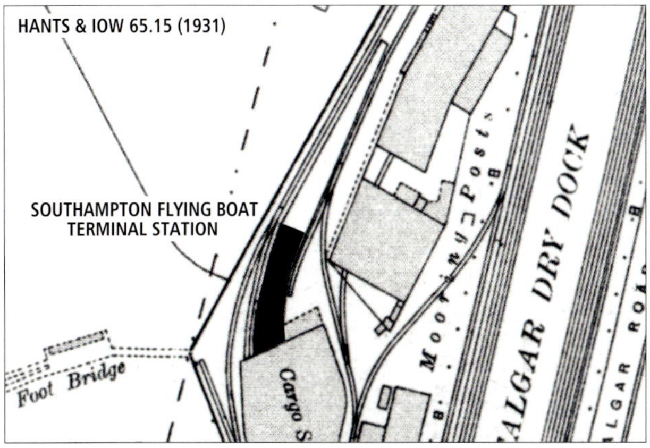

SOUTHAMPTON OCEAN TERMINAL

Opened in 1966 by BR and closed 14 December 1991.

Line lifted Demolished Station site in dock use
SU42408 10356

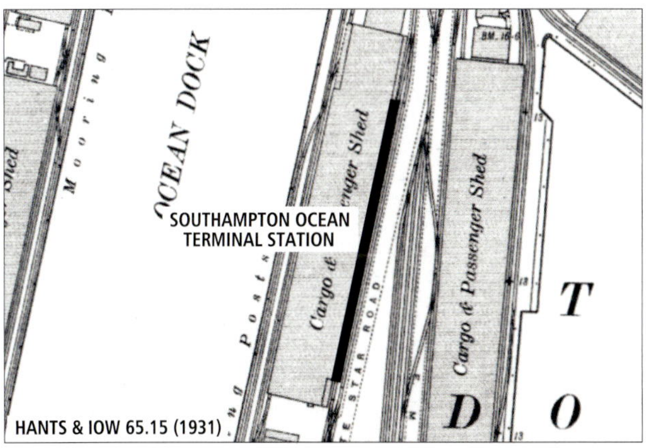

SOUTHAMPTON ROYAL PIER

Opened 26 September 1871 by the L&SWR and closed 1 October 1914.

Line lifted – Demolished – Pier derelict – Station site unused **SU41748 10882**

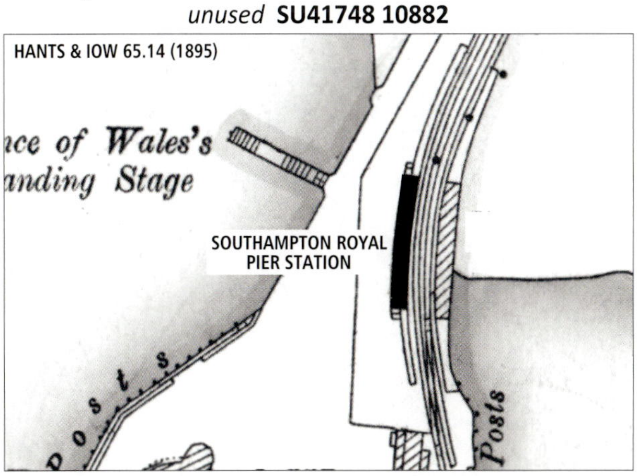

SOUTHAMPTON TERMINUS

Opened 11 May 1840 by the L&SWR as *Southampton*, renamed as *Southampton Docks* in 1858, as *Southampton Town & Dock* in 1896, as *Southampton Town for Docks* in 1912, as *Southampton Terminus for Docks* 9 July 1923 by the SR, as *Southampton Terminus* in 1955 by BR and closed 5 September 1966.

Line lifted – Demolished – Station site occupied by a car park and housing in Captains Place **SU42562 11072**

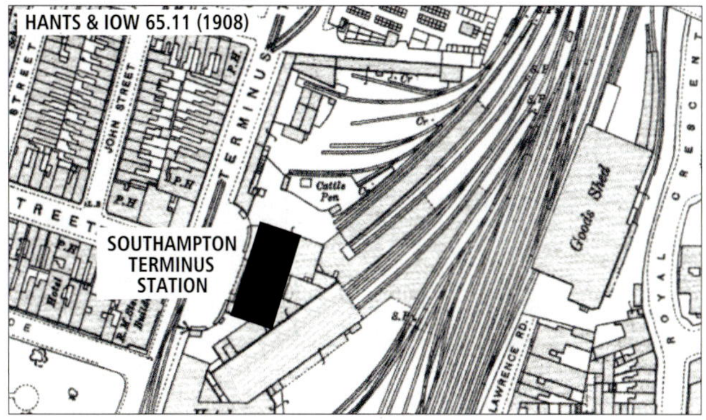

SOUTHAMPTON WEST END

Opened 1 June 1847 by the Southampton & Dorchester Railway as *Southampton Blechynden*, renamed as *Southampton West End* in 1858 by the L&SWR and closed 1 November 1895.

Line Operational – Demolished – Part of station site occupied by Southampton Central Station Car Park
SU41462 12160

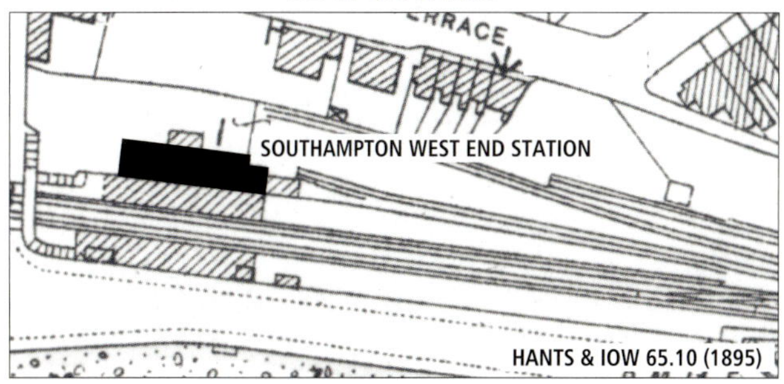

STOKES BAY

Opened 6 April 1863 by the Stokes Bay Railway & Pier and closed 1 November 1915 by the L&SWR.

Line lifted – Pier and station demolished **SZ59991 97875**

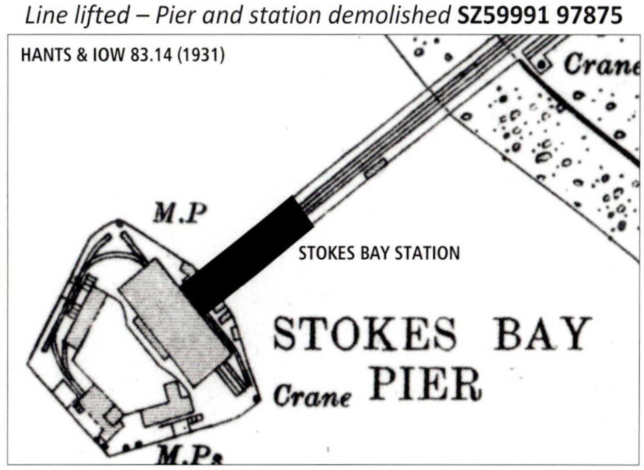

SWANWICK

Opened 2 September 1889 by the L&SWR.

SU51760 08725

Viewed on 2 October 2015

WARBLINGTON

Opened 1 November 1907 by the LB&SCR as *Denville Halt* renamed as *Warblington Halt* in December 1907 and as *Warblington* 5 May 1969 by BR.

SU72824 06504

Viewed on 1 October 2016

SWAYTHLING

Opened 15 October 1883 by the L&SWR as *Swathling* and renamed as *Swaythling* 1 June 1895.

SU43912 15941

Viewed on 3 October 2015

WELLINGTON COLLEGE

Opened 29 January 1859 by the SER and closed c1860.

Line Operational – Demolished – No access

SU82562 63023 (a)

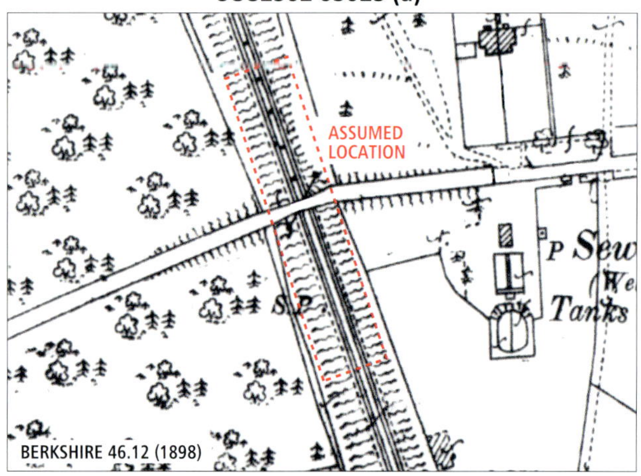

BERKSHIRE 46.12 (1898)

TISTED

Opened 1 June 1903 by the L&SWR as *Tisted*, renamed as *Tisted for Selborne* in 1914, reverted to *Tisted* in 1927 by the SR and closed 7 February 1955 by BR.

Line lifted – Station building in private use **SU70694 32221**

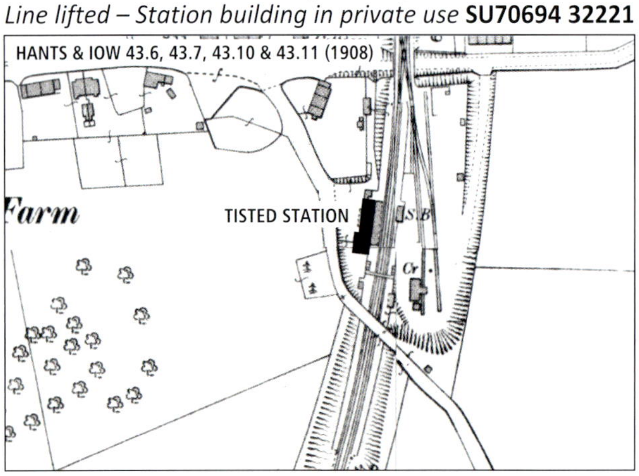

HANTS & IOW 43.6, 43.7, 43.10 & 43.11 (1908)

WEST MEON

Opened 1 June 1903 by the L&SWR and closed 7 February 1955 by BR.

Line lifted – Demolished – Degraded platforms extant – Station site unused **SU64245 23656**

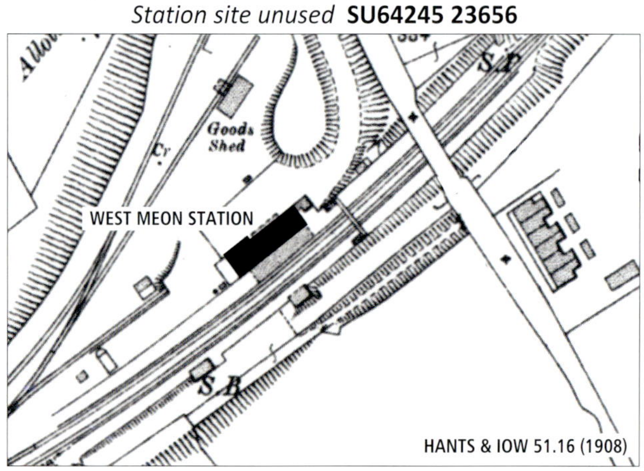

HANTS & IOW 51.16 (1908)

WHITCHURCH (Hampshire)

Opened 3 July 1854 by the L&SWR as *Whitchurch*, renamed as *Whitchurch North* 26 September 1949 by BR and as *Whitchurch (Hampshire)* 2 October 1972.

SU46338 48918

Viewed on 3 October 2015

WINCHFIELD

Opened 24 September 1838 by the London & Southampton Railway as *Shapley Heath* and renamed as *Winchfield* c1840 by the L&SWR.

SU76311 54523

Viewed on 9 July 2017

WICKHAM

Opened 1 June 1903 by the L&SWR and closed 7 February 1955 by BR.

Line lifted – Demolished - Platforms extant - The Meon Valley Trail passes through the station site

SU57543 11771

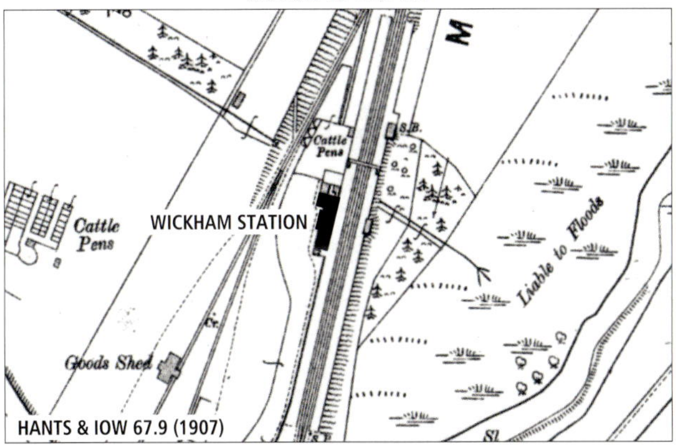

HANTS & IOW 67.9 (1907)

WINNERSH

Opened 1 January 1910 by the SE&CR as *Sindlesham & Hurst Halt*, renamed as *Winnersh Halt* 6 July 1930 by the SR and as *Winnersh* 5 May 1969 by BR.

SU78158 70756

Viewed on 16 April 2017

WINCHESTER

Opened 10 June 1839 by the London & Southampton Railway as *Winchester*, renamed as *Winchester City* 26 September 1949 by BR and reverted to *Winchester* 10 July 1967. **SU47747 30005**

Viewed on 3 October 2015

WINNERSH TRIANGLE

Opened 12 May 1986 by BR.

SU77141 71439

Viewed on 16 April 2017

WOKINGHAM

Opened 4 July 1849 by the Reading, Guildford & Reigate Railway. **SU80565 68734**

Viewed on 16 April 2017

WOOLSTON

Opened 5 March 1866 by the Southampton & Netley Railway

SU43904 11247

Viewed on 3 October 2015

BIBLIOGRAPHY

Railway Atlas Then and Now by Paul Smith & Keith Turner Crécy Publishing Third Edition (2020). ISBN 978-0-86093-698-5

Railway Passenger Stations in Great Britain: A Chronology by Michael Quick. Railway & Canal Historical Society (2009) ISBN 978-0-901461-57-5

The Directory of Railway Stations by RVJ Butt. Patrick Stephens Ltd (1995). ISBN 1-85260-508-1

British Railway Stations 1825-1900: An Essential Gazetteer by Paul Smith & Sally Salmon. Unique Books (2023) ISBN 978-1-913555-15-3

British Railway Stations Since 1901: An Essential Gazetteer by Paul Smith & Sally Salmon. Unique Books (2022) ISBN 978-1-913555-11-5

WEBSITES ACCESSED

Disused Stations: http://disused-stations.org.uk/
National Library of Scotland: www.nls.uk

Maps sourced from the Cambridge University Map Library are reproduced by permission of the Syndics of Cambridge University.

The Up side of Alresford station recorded from a service train on 17 September 1972.
Geoffrey Tribe/Online Transport Archive

Two Rebuilt Bulleid Pacifics — Nos 34087 *145 Squadron* and 34004 *Yeovil* — await departure with Down services from Basingstoke on 6 September 1966. *Rev A. M. Logan/Online Transport Archive*

A three-car DMU departs from Crowthorne with the 11.5am service from Reading South on 29 April 1961. *Alexander McBlain/Online Transport Archive*

Left: **The experimental Sadler railcar is pictured at Droxford station post closure.** *Harry Luff/Online Transport Archive*

Below: **Ex-GWR 0-6-0 No 2240 stands at Eastleigh with the 2.12pm to Newbury on 27 January 1960.** *Alexander McBlain/Online Transport Archive*

The exterior of Farnborough (Main) station on 23 April 1965. *Alexander McBlain/Online Transport Archive*

On 3 May 1953 'Terrier' No 32677 is pictured on Hayling Island duties at Havant. *John McCann/Online Transport Archive*

Langston Halt on 8 June 1963. *Gerald Druce/Online Transport Archive*

Two 2-6-2Ts — Nos 41328 and 82012 — pass through Millbrook with an oil train from Fawley on 19 September 1962. *Alexander McBlain/Online Transport Archive*

North Hayling Halt on 8 June 1963. *Gerald Druce/Online Transport Archive*

DEMU No 1105 at Portsmouth Harbour on 4 May 1978. *Geoffrey Tribe/Online Transport Archive*

DEMU No 1115 and Class 4VEP No 7787 at Portsmouth & Southsea on 4 May 1978. *Geoffrey Tribe/Online Transport Archive*

Ivatt 2-6-2T No 41293 heads a rake of empty oil wagons for Fawley on 29 September 1961 at Southampton Central. *Alexander McBlain/Online Transport Archive*

The exterior of Southampton Terminus station on 4 April 1970. *Geoffrey Tribe/Online Transport Archive*

Type 3 (Class 37) No 6722 passes through Winchester with a Down Freightliner service on 23 June 1973. *Geoffrey Tribe/Online Transport Archive*

An undated 1948 view — although it cannot be any earlier than May that year as it only acquired its BR number that month — sees 'N' Class No 31873 departing from Romsey. *Tony Wickens/Online Transport Archive*

Classic Tours

LCGB 'Somerset & Dorset' 30 September 1962

Photographs: Les Collings/Online Transport Archive

On 30 September 1962 the Locomotive Club of Great Britain organised its 'Somerset & Dorset' rail tour. This was designed to take passengers out from London Waterloo, along the main line to Southampton and then access the Somerset & Dorset at Broadstone. Having reached Bath Green Park, ex-Midland Railway metals were then used to take the train to Bristol Temple Meads for a return to Paddington via Badminton, Swindon and Didcot.

The scheduled departure from Waterloo was at 9.12am behind 'Battle of Britain' No 34064 *Fighter Command*, which was booked to take the train as far as Broadstone via Wimborne. Although a few minutes were lost in the Down direction, Broadstone was reached at just after 11.54am (just over 10 minutes late). With No 34064 removed, one of the S&D's 2-8-0s — No 53808 — was coupled up for the northbound journey to Evercreech Junction. The train now departed 13 minutes late, at 12.9pm rather than the booked 11.56am, but some smart running meant that two minutes of this had been regained by Evercreech Junction, which

For the outward journey from London Waterloo to Broadstone, via Southampton and Ringwood, Unrebuilt 'Battle of Britain' No 34064 *Fighter Command* was employed. The locomotive and its train are pictured here at Waterloo shortly before its scheduled 9.1am departure time.

Wimborne, where No 34064 and the train are recorded here, was reached late — 11.36am as opposed to a scheduled 11.30am — and was also to see a late departure — just after 11.44am rather than the booked 11.39am.

The special included a return trip from Evercreech Junction to Burnham-on-Sea; for this section of the excursion the motive power was Collett-designed 0-6-0 No 3210 and here the train is recorded at Glastonbury & Street on its outward journey. The special spent just under 10 minutes here, from 1.55pm to just before 2.4pm, before continuing its journey westwards. By this date the locomotive had been based on the S&D for almost two years, having been reallocated to Templecombe from Croes Newydd in the late autumn of 1960. It was to be withdrawn from Templecombe in late November 1964.

was reached at 1.23pm rather than the booked 1.4pm. At Evercreech Junction, ex-GWR 0-6-0 No 3210 was coupled up to take the train via Glastonbury and Highbridge to Burnham-on-Sea. By this date regular timetabled services over the section from Highbridge to Burnham had been withdrawn — as from 29 October 1951 — but occasional specials and excursions had operated over the line since then. This traffic ceased, however, in 1961 although the line itself was to remain open for goods traffic until freight facilities were withdrawn from Burnham-on-Sea on 20 May 1963.

The booked arrival time at Burnham was 2.12pm but it was not until 2.35pm that the special finally reached its destination and more time was lost whilst the locomotive ran round its train. The special departed at 2.46pm, rather than the booked 2.23pm, but some of this late running was recovered by curtailing the booked stop at Highbridge from 27 minutes to 18 minutes with the result that the train headed back to Evercreech Junction at just after 3.10pm, some 15 minutes down. However, this good work was more than lost during the return trip to Evercreech Junction, where the trip took 58 minutes rather than the booked 42, with the result that the special arrived at just after 4.8pm rather than the scheduled 3.37pm.

At Evercreech Junction No 53808 was reattached to the train but the operation cost a further five minute delay with the result that the special did not depart until just after 4.21pm rather than the booked 3.45pm. The train was now running more than half-an-hour late. Further time was lost on the next section with the result that arrival at Bath Green Park was not until just after 5.33pm (as opposed to the scheduled 4.46pm). At Bath Green Park 0-6-0 No 44558 was rostered to take the special to Bristol Temple Meads; unfortunately, further time was lost at Green Park with the result that the train departed at 5.46pm rather than 4.56pm. A further minute was lost on this section of the trip, with arrival at Temple Meads being made at 6.8pm rather than 5.38pm. From Temple Meads to Paddington ex-GWR 2-8-0 No 4704 was booked to haul the train but a further seven minutes were lost prior to departure. However, just after 6.28pm (as opposed to the booked 5.50pm), the service departed. The crew of the 2-8-0 was clearly determined to try and pick up some of the lost time and, by the time that it passed through Swindon, the delay had been reduced to only 33 minutes (7.30pm rather than the booked 6.57pm).

However, the locomotive had possibly been pushed too hard with the result that it developed a hot box between Swindon and Didcot, with the train passing through Steventon at 8pm (against a scheduled 7.20pm) and an unscheduled stop at Didcot at 8.8pm (rather than passing through non-stop at 7.23pm) saw No 4707 removed and replaced by 'County' class 4-6-0 No 1007 *County of Brecknock*. The replacement of the locomotive resulted in a further 12 minute delay, with the train finally departing for Paddington at 8.20pm. Sadly this was not the final delay to the train; booked to complete the journey from Didcot to Paddington in 62 minutes, the 'County' actually took 75 minutes, arriving at its destination at 9.35pm, 70 minutes down on the booked arrival time.

Although closed to regular passenger services on 29 October 1951, Burnham-on-Sea continued to receive summer excursion trains until early September 1962. By the date of the LCGB special, final closure of the line from Highbridge was fast approaching; freight facilities were withdrawn from the station on 20 May 1963. The special made a 10-minute stop, between 2.35pm and 2.46pm, whilst the locomotive ran round the train before heading back towards Evercreech Junction.

On the return journey to Evercreech Junction the train made an 18-minute stop at Highbridge, between 2.52pm and just after 3.10pm. The brief pause allowed passengers to explore the engine and the site of the erstwhile Somerset & Dorset workshops.

Heading north from Evercreech Junction to Bath, the train paused for eight minutes — rather than the booked 10 — between 4.42pm and 4.50pm at Shepton Mallet during which time it was possible to record this view of Charlton Viaduct looking towards the north. There were three viaducts at Shepton Mallet of which Charlton — with its 27 arches — was the longest at 317 yards. Originally constructed for single track, the viaduct was rebuilt in 1892 when the line between Shepton Mallet and Binegar was doubled. The viaduct survives today and is now listed Grade II*.

Viewed from the train, Bath Green Park shed was still a hive of activity. The first part of the shed to open was the two-road stone built shed on the south side of the site; this was opened by the Midland Railway on 4 August 1869. The Somerset & Dorset shed — a wooden-built structure — on the north side first opened on 20 July 1874 and was extended twice, once in 1878 and again in 1884. In 1935 the facilities at the shed were further enhanced by the provision of a 60ft turntable. The shed closed with the demise of the Somerset & Dorset and the ex-Midland line to Bristol on 7 March 1966.

The onward journey from Bath Green Park to Bristol Temple Meads was in the hands of Fowler-designed Class 4F 0-6-0 No 44558. This particular member of the class was allocated to Bath Green Park shed for its entire career post-nationalisation; it was to remain in service until withdrawal in mid-December 1964. By the time that the train departed from Bath Green Park at 5.46pm it was some 50 minutes late, its booked departure having been 4.56pm.

The booked locomotive for the return trip from Bristol Temple Meads to Paddington was Southall-allocated, Churchward-designed 2-8-0 No 4707, pictured here at Bristol prior to departure. Scheduled to head east at 5.50pm, the train actually departed at just after 6.28pm. Unfortunately, during the course of the journey, No 4707 ran a hot box and had to be removed from the train at Didcot; it was replaced there by 'County' class 4-6-0 No 1007 *County of Brecknock*, which resulted in the train not arriving at its final destination until 9.35pm — some 70 minutes late.

Class 419 Motor Luggage Vans

There cannot be many types of traction that have seen 80% survive in some guise more than 60 years after they were introduced but that's the status of the Class 419 Motor Luggage Vans that were introduced following the Kent Coast Electrification scheme.

The origins of the 10 single units constructed lay in the construction of a single parcels unit — No E68000 — for the North Eastern Region's third-rail network on Tyneside. This unit was constructed at Eastleigh in 1955 to Diagram No 499. Tested on the Southern following delivery on 29 October 1955, the unit was transferred to Tyneside in January 1956, where it was based at South Gosforth. However, its time in north-east England was short as the Tyneside third-rail units were replaced by DMUs in the early 1960s and, following this, No E68000 was transferred to the Merseyside third-rail network where, renumbered M68000, it was based at Southport from August 1963 for use on the line to Liverpool. However, its sojourn on the LMR was even shorter than that on the NER; it was stored prior to being officially withdrawn in March 1967. It was scrapped later the same year, ironically returning to the north-east for disposal.

Recognising the fact that the Kent Coast electrification scheme also involved trains to and from the ports of Dover and Folkestone and thus potentially liable to carry significant quantities of luggage for the cross-channel ferry services, 10 Motor Luggage Vans (MLVs) were ordered as part of the project. The first pair, S68001 and S68002 (Lot No 30458) , were ordered as part of the first phase of the scheme in February 1957. The remaining eight — Nos S68003-10 (Lot No 30623) — were ordered in July 1959 in connection with the second phase of the scheme. The first two were delivered in May 1959 and the remainder in late 1960 and early 1961.

It's 3 March 1961 and Nos S68005 and S68004, when virtually brand new, are pictured running under battery power towards the quayside at Dover Marine having formed part of the 9am boat train from Victoria to Dover that connected with a steamer service to Ostend. *M. Edwards*

68001
74
5
Tickets

On 15 June 1984 No 68010 brings up the rear of a service departing from Folkestone Harbour station. *Bernard Harrison/Online Transport Archive*

All 10 were constructed at Eastleigh Works on frames fabricated at Ashford. Unlike No E68000, which had two powered bogies, the units constructed for the Southern had only one (which was fitted with two English Electric 250hp motors). Designed for use on the third-rail system, the 10 vehicles were also equipped with batteries for use on non-electrified sections — such as sidings at Dover — with protective measures taken to ensure that, when operating in battery mode, the shoes for the third rail were raised.

Following the delivery of the first pair in May 1959, the duo underwent tests before the launch of the initial electric services on 15 June 1959. Whilst their primary purpose was to provide additional luggage accommodation on the services to and from the Channel ports, the new units — being self-propelled — also found themselves employed on a range of dedicated parcels duties, plus other work, and this increased with the arrival of the second batch in 1960/61.

The early years of the Kent Coast electric services to the Channel ports often saw the quantity of luggage carried exceed the capacity of a single MLV — this was a problem given the use of more than one MLV in multiple with a 12-car rake of passenger EMUs was approaching the maximum power requirement that the electrical equipment could support — and so it was decided to produce a batch of six Trailer Luggage Vans; Nos S68201-06 were converted from Mark I BG vans during 1968. These were unpowered and lacked driving cabs; consequently, the TLVs caused problems over their definition — were they, for example, to be regarded as a hauled vehicle or a multiple-unit? — and debate with the unions. The decline in luggage carried, however, rendered the debate increasingly irrelevant as the trailers were surplus to requirements as a single MLV could handle what traffic there remained.

From the early 1970s, as the requirements for their use on the services to the Channel ports declined, the MLVs increasingly found themselves utilised on other traffic; this included parcels traffic on the Central Division. However, this work highlighted a potential problem with the braking that led to a number of signals being over-run and, in April 1985, a slow-speed collision with the buffers at London Bridge. In order to counter this the braking system on the MLVs was modified at Selhurst; whilst this work was being completed, the units could only operate in multiple. Another modification — completed between March 1984 and December 1985 — saw all 10 units equipped with AWS.

Opposite top: **On 9 July 1973 parcels are loaded on board No 68004 at Dover Marine. All 10 of the units were repainted into blue and grey livery between February 1968 and September 1970; No 68004 was the last to emerge with No 68003 being the first.** *Geoffrey Tribe/Online Transport Archive*

Bottom: **Pictured at Dover Western Docks on 23 July 1983, the first of the Southern units — No 68001 — is about to depart with the 16.16 service to London Victoria via Faversham. The remainder of the train comprises two Class 4VEP units: Nos 7872 and 7892.** *Alex Dasi-Sutton*

Awaiting their next duties at Dover Marine on 14 September 1984 are Nos 68002 and 68010. The former was scheduled to be repainted in Post Office red in early 1989 — indeed work was partially completed at Selhurst — when, on 8 March 1989, one of the two units already repainted — No 9004 (the other being No 9001) — was held up and robbed at Merstham. The decision was taken that the red livery made the units too conspicuous with the result that the red livery was abandoned and No 9002 — as the unit had been renumbered — emerged in full Network SouthEast livery in June that year.
Bernard Harrison/Online Transport Archive

The MLVs were initially allocated Class 422 under the TOPS scheme; this was amended to Class 419. They were also the only BR stock to be classified both as a locomotive and as a multiple-unit. Reflecting the TOPS scheme, in early 1987 the 10 vehicles were allocated unit numbers, becoming Nos 9001-10 in sequence. With the development of the Sectors, the majority of the MLVs were allocated to the Parcels Sector; this resulted in two appearing in Post Office red livery (with others scheduled to receive it). This was, however, short-lived as the colour scheme highlighted the use to which the stock was employed and led to a robbery in March 1989 when a Brighton to London Bridge working was targeted at Merstham. The red livery was abandoned as a consequence.

By the time that Network SouthEast — to which the vehicles were allocated — was created in 1986, the MLVs were rapidly losing their diagrammed work. In May 1990, the Royal Mail ceased to use trains on the former Southern Region for the movement of post, and cross-channel business rarely required their use, and the batch found itself used largely for shunting purposes. Half the batch — Nos 9003/07-10 — were in store by the summer of 1990. These, with the exception of 9010, were officially withdrawn in May 1991; Nos 9001 and 9005 were withdrawn at the same time. Nos 9002/04/06/10 were officially withdrawn in September 1991. All 10 were transferred to departmental stock but No 9006 was not to last long on these duties, being withdrawn three months later following a collision.

Opposite: **In 1985 and 1986 four of the units — Nos 68001/03/05/08 — were painted in the first London South East Sector livery of two-tone brown and orange (the so-called 'Jaffa Cake' livery). One of this quartet — No 68005 — is pictured at Dover Marine on 1 August 1986.**
Geoffrey Tribe/Online Transport Archive

Private
68005

On 15 March 1986 No 68007 is pictured at Folkestone with an Up boat train from Dover Western Docks to Victoria. No 68007 had been repainted into the blue and grey livery in January 1970 but was not to retain it for long after being recorded here. In early 1987 the MLV started to carry the unit's number 9007 and was repainted into the second version of the London South East sector livery — with the thin black lines above and below the orange stripe at, probably, the same time. *Alex Dasi-Sutton*

By the late 1980s many of the MLVs were working on postal services conveying Royal Mail traffic. As a result it was decided to repaint the units into red and brand them 'Royal Mail'. The first to be so treated was No 9004 in October 1988; this was followed by No 9001 in February 1989. The latter is illustrated here at London Bridge on 25 March 1989 looking bright in its newly applied livery. However, by this date the new livery had already shown itself to be a problem when, on 8 March 1989, thieves targeted No 9004 in an armed robbery at Merstham. Both Nos 9001 and 9004 — along with partially repainted No 9002 — were speedily repainted into Network SouthEast livery. *Alex Dasi-Sutton*

MLV

Original No.	New No.	Renumbered (first) & when	Renumbered (second)	AWS fitted	Withdrawn	Fate	Notes
68000	October 1955	N/A	N/A	N/A	March 1967	Scrapped August 1967	
68001	April 1959	9001 February 1987	931091 (also carried 091)	July 1985		Preserved 1998	
68002	May 1959	9002 March 1987	931092	March 1984		Preserved 2004	
68003	December 1960	9003 March 1987	(931093) Not physically renumbered	November 1984		Preserved 2000	
68004	December 1960	9004 February 1987	931094	April 1985		Preserved 2004	Victim of robbery at Merstham on 8 March 1989 when painted in distinctive red Post Office livery
68005	January 1961	9005	XXXX	931095	January 1986		Preserved 2000
68006	January 1961	9006 March 1987	N/A	December 1985	December 1991	Scrapped March 1994	Withdrawn as result of collision with Class 4CEP No 1559 on 6 December 1991 at Ramsgate
68007	February 1961	N/A	931097	April 1984		Initially acquired in 2000 but scrapped November 2006	Purchased for spares and eventually scrapped at Coventry
68008	March 1961	9008 March 1987	931098	July 1986		Preserved 2000	
68009	March 1961	9009 March 1987	(931099) Not physically renumbered	April 1984		Preserved 2000	
68010	March 1961	9010 March 1987	931090	June 1985		Preserved 2000	

TLVs	Converted	Original BG No.	Withdrawn	Departmental No.	Departmental allocation	Fate
68201	1968	80915	August 1976	ADB975611	Old Oak Common	Scrapped September 2011
68202	1968	80918	August 1976	ADB975613	Old Oak Common	Scrapped September 2011
68203	1968	80922	August 1976	ADB975612	Cardiff Canton	Scrapped September 2011
68204	1968	80925	August 1976	ADB975614	Bristol Bath Road	Scrapped March 1996
68205	1968	80942	August 1976	ADB975610	Bristol Bath Road	Scrapped March 1996
68206	1968	80951	August 1976	ADB975615	Plymouth Laira	Scrapped January 1998

The surviving nine vehicles were notionally renumbered 931091-95/97-99/90 although not all were to carry the new number. At privatisation, the nine vehicles — although effectively redundant (despite efforts to try and find new work for them) — were transferred to the ownership of Porterbrook. Eight of the units were concentrated in store at Ashford in May 1986; the following month these, along with the ninth vehicle (No 931091) were moved to Strawberry Hill where they were examined for possible conversion into Sandite units for use on Merseyside. This was not pursued, however, and later the same month the nine vehicles were moved once again, this time to Bournemouth where they were to remain in store for at least a further two years.

The first to be sold was No 931091 (68001) which passed to the EPB Preservation Group during the summer of 1998. It was based on the East Kent Railway at Shepherdswell where it operated in conjunction with the group's preserved Class 2EPB No 5739. Also based for a period on the EKR was No 68002; this was restored to service as a depot shunter at Bournemouth in late 1998 and was transferred to the EKR in early 2004. In early 2000 a further six units were disposed of; Nos 68003/04 went initially to the Mid-Norfolk Railway, whilst 68005/08 moved to Coventry (where they were subsequently joined by No 68007, which was scrapped for spares in late 2006) and Nos 68009/10 were transferred to the Colne Valley Railway. Subsequently No 68003 was sold and transferred to Warcop for use on the Eden Valley Railway where it was eventually joined by No 68005. Also based for some time on the EKR were Nos 68008, which was relocated there in September 2007, and 68009, which followed two years later. Finally, No 68010 was based for a period on the Wensleydale Railway.

At the time of writing Nos 68001/02/08/09 are stored at Southall with Nos 68003/05/10 on the Eden Valley Railway, where No 68010 has been converted into a shop, and No 68004 is in use on the Mid-Norfolk Railway.

Only three of the class were repainted into the new Network SouthEast livery; Nos 9001/02/04 were to emerge bearing the revised brand in June and July 1989 following the decision to abandon the red Royal Mail branding. On 29 July 1989 No 9004, freshly repainted, is seen at South Croydon with a mail service from London Bridge. *Alex Dasi-Sutton*

Just before 1pm on 15 March 1990 two vehicles — Nos 9007 and 9010 — are pictured being loaded in London Bridge station. The two are wearing the second version of the London South East Sector livery, where, in contrast to the earlier version, the orange band is now bordered by a thin black line. Of the 10 vehicles, again only four — Nos 9006/07/09/10 — carried this livery, which was first applied to No 68009 in July 1986. By the early 1990s, the MLVs were approaching the end of their revenue earning career; the first vehicles to go into store were Nos 9003/07-10 by the middle of the year. *Gavin Morrison*

A Day in the Life

Photographs Bernard Harrison/ Bob Bridger Collection/Online Transport Archive

By the summer of 1965 only one part of Great Britain saw its passenger services provided exclusively by steam traction — the Isle of Wight — and on Saturday 28 August Bernard Harrison spent the day recording scenes on the line from Ryde Pier Head to Ventnor. By this date only some 15 of the Class O2s on which services had largely relied post-nationalisation remained in service and this number was further reduced the following month when No W30 *Shorwell* was withdrawn.

The day started in Ryde where the first train to be photographed saw No W26 *Whitwell* awaiting departure from Ryde Esplanade with the 8.39am service from Shanklin to Ryde Pier Head.

Although the railways on the island owed most of their infrastructure and equipment to the 19th century, more modern transport was also present in the guise of the hovercraft service from Southsea and Gosport to Ryde. Pictured at Ryde is one of the two SR.N6 hovercraft that had been leased by Hovertravel in 1965 and 1966 for use on the route. The first — numbered 130/GH2013 — had only commenced operation the previous month. This particular craft was to survive in service until 1980.

Opposite: Post-nationalisation, two additional members of the 'O2' class were shipped across the Solent to supplement the fleet on the island. One of these — No W35 *Freshwater* — is seen here heading south from Pier Head station with the 9.10am service to Shanklin. Whilst No W36 *Carisbrooke* had already been withdrawn by this date — although it was still extant as it was not scrapped until October 1965 — No W35 survived until the end of steam-hauled passenger services.

Bottom: Heading north near Smallbrook Junction with the 9.47am service from Sandown to Ryde Pier Head is No W16 *Ventnor*. This was another of the class that remained in service until passenger services were suspended to facilitate the electrification of the line from Ryde Pier Head to Shanklin.

Heading north near Smallbrook Junction with t
that remained in service until passenger service

A panoramic view of Ventnor station sees No W35 again, this time awaiting departure from Ventnor with the 12.20pm service to Ryde Pier Head. There is evidence of freight traffic in the yard; by this date, however, the days of goods trains to Ventnor were drawing to a close — freight facilities were withdrawn from the station on 4 October 1965.

No W35 has got the signal and is seen departing from Ventnor with the 12.20pm service to Ryde Pier Head.

Heading north, the photographer captured the 12.40pm service from Ventnor to Ryde Pier Head near Shanklin. The locomotive was No W26 *Whitwell*.

A further northbound service — the 1.12pm from Shanklin to Ryde Pier Head behind No W22 *Brading* — was the next train to be recorded. It is seen here just to the north of Shanklin station. No W22 was another of the class to survive until the end of steam operation on the island.

The final view of the day saw No W35 *Freshwater* depart with the 3.10pm service to Ventnor.

Opposite: Having recorded two northbound services near Shanklin, the next train to be photographed was the 1.10pm southbound service from Ryde Pier Head to Ventnor which was hauled on this occasion by No W30 *Shorwell*. These must have been amongst the last of the duties that No W30 undertook as it was to be withdrawn from service during the week ending 12 September 1965 but was not finally to be cut up until more than two years later.

Bottom: After completing his photography at Shanklin, Bernard Harrison headed back to Ryde for his final photographs of the day. The first of these was to record No W26 *Whitwell* heading towards Pier Head station with the 2.31pm service from Sandown.

Index of Locations

Corrigenda

With thanks to both Brian McCarthy and David Hodge, the origin of Breamore, Downton, Fordingbridge and Verwood was the Salisbury & Dorset Railway and not the Somerset & Dorset.

David also noticed that somehow Wherwell station was omitted from the feature on stations; that omission is rectified with the block alongside. It should have also appeared on the key map between Longparish and Fullerton. He also notes that Lake station, whilst appearing in the text, is omitted from the key map; for reference it should have been located between Sandown and Shanklin stations on the Isle of Wight. Unfortunately, the captions for the lower image on page 15 and the upper on page 16 have been transposed. In the caption referring to the upper image on page 68, the locomotive featured in the image is No 33022; the locomotive is incorrectly referred to as No 33021 later in the caption. Finally, on page 91 No 73083 is of course a Class 5 not Class 4 and the train is heading for Bournemouth Central and not Waterloo.

As always, please forward on any comments or corrections by either email or by letter; they're all gratefully received.

WHERWELL

Opened 1 June 1885 by the L&SWR and closed 6 July 1931 by the SR.

Line lifted – Station building in private use – Remainder of station site occupied by dwellings in Chant Close

SU38784 40858

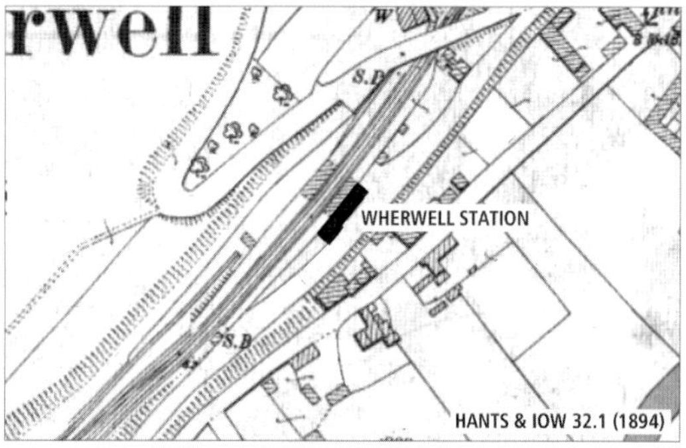